"Read Rosalyn Berne."

— Rita Mae Brown, MFH, author

series, and the *Snea*~~~~ *~ ~ ~rown* mystery series

"I first experienced Rosalyn's gifts while in Costa Rica leading a workshop on equine facilitated psychotherapy. I saw her from a distance in the barn, doing what looked like petting a horse. Little did I know that there was much more going on: I watched Rosalyn nodding her head as she spoke to the horse named Beauty, not with words out loud but in a language I can only describe as two beings communicating at a cellular level. I had never witnessed this before, although I'd heard of animal communication, and had even worked with some of the best. But this was different: I saw Beauty toss her head, then be still. As I approached, I could hear Rosalyn saying to Beauty 'Tell me more about this.' I sensed that Beauty was saying, '. . . stay here Rosalyn, I have so much to tell you.'

"I was there to teach an apprenticeship class on equine facilitated learning and psychotherapy with Dr. Nancy Coyne. I asked Rosalyn to spend an afternoon with my apprentices so they could experience how she worked; none of them had ever met or spoken to Rosalyn. We sat in a circle in the arena: eight students, Rosalyn, and three other instructors. Rosalyn asked for Beauty and Dorado to walk free in the arena while she worked. She started with a moment of silence, creating a space of meditative stillness. In the silence, I watched my students get emotional. One student who had never expressed any emotion had tears streaming down her face. Rosalyn asked if anyone had any questions; this woman spoke up, asking Rosalyn if she would ever be able to forgive herself, not saying for what she needed forgiveness. We knew some details about this situation, but Rosalyn had had no knowledge of it. This student had been living in anguished guilt for seventeen years over losing her child in an accident. As Rosalyn spoke to her, Beauty walked right behind the student, and began licking and chewing with her tongue and teeth; when horses do this, it signifies they are with a person who is speaking from their heart. The horse never lies; Beauty was telling Rosalyn to keep speaking, sensing this woman needed help. Rosalyn described the incident in detail as it had happened, while also translating an important message from Beauty: '. . . Beauty wants to say that you need not grieve for this soul; every soul has a purpose, and the purpose of that soul was to save your life. Your work was not done . . . you need only celebrate and be grateful for that soul.' This student had been kicked in the belly when eight months pregnant; the baby's head stopped the kick from causing fatal internal injuries, but the baby died instantly.

"None of us will forget that tearful, healing, miraculous day. I witnessed tears of grief transform to tears of relief and then to joy as we watched this miracle of equine healing unfold."

—Shelley Rosenberg, author of
My Horses, My Healers and *Accessing Your Intuition*

WAKING
TO
BEAUTY

Books by Rosalyn Berne

When the Horses Whisper:
The Wisdom of Wise and Sentient Beings

Nanotalk: Conversations with Scientists
and Engineers about Ethics, Meaning, and
Belief in the Development of Nanotechnology

Waiting in the Silence

Creating Life from Life:
Biotechnology and Science Fiction

WAKING

TO

BEAUTY

Encounters with Remarkable Beings

ROSALYN W. BERNE

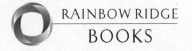

RAINBOW RIDGE
BOOKS

Cover and interior design by Frame25 Productions
Cover photograph by Sandy Sharkey (*www.sandysharkey.com*)

Published by:
Rainbow Ridge Books, LLC
140 Rainbow Ridge Road
Faber. Virginia 22938
www.rainbowridgebooks.com
434-361-1723

If you are unable to order this book from your local
bookseller, you may order directly from the distributor.

Square One Publishers, Inc.
115 Herricks Road
Garden City Park, NY 11040
Phone: (516) 535-2010
Fax: (516) 535-2014
Toll-free: 877-900-BOOK

Visit the author at:
www.rosalynberne.com
and
www.whenthehorseswhisper.com

Library of Congress Cataloging-in-Publication Data applied for.

ISBN 978-1-937907-40-2

10 9 8 7 6 5 4 3 2 1

Printed on acid-free paper in Canada

Dedicated to Barbara Rose Troncoso

Contents

Introduction

ONE DAY RECENTLY, sitting in the Blue Ridge Mountain cabin in Virginia where my husband and I go to retreat and write, something (I consider it to be the "still small voice") prompted me to look up from my work and out the picture window. "Don't be afraid," the voice said as I gazed at the distant blue ridges. "Trust what you sense and allow yourself to feel it." I moved the computer aside and walked outside onto the grass. Everything around me took on a shimmering quality of aliveness. The trees, the plants, the grass, the sky, the air, and even the rocks, all seemed to be vibrating, albeit subtly, with a presence permeating it all. For a moment I panicked, alarmed at this sudden shift in awareness. Then I realized: *The life force is everywhere.*

This is not a book I intended to write. Its contents include personal experiences that I never planned to share publically. I earn my living as a scholar, studying and writing about bioethics, and the implications of emerging technologies for humanity and the earth. My work environment is a university engineering school, where the focus is on that which can be detected, observed, measured, predicted, replicated, designed, and built, using tested formulas and proven equations of the scientific method. It is an institution oriented around concrete understandings of the material world. In contrast to that, much of what I've written here is unfathomable. But when prompted to write about these experiences by one I consider to be a wise being, I said yes; so here is the sequel to *When the Horses Whisper*.

This book recounts elements of my life that continue to move and change me in profound ways. Many of the experiences described here have altered my sense of what life is, what God is, and who I am as a human being. I hope what I have written will hearten those who read it, because we are living in particularly trying times, with dramatically changing outer conditions on the planet, and the inner "great turning" of human consciousness. For much of my life I was oriented somewhere "out there," absorbed with otherworldly, religious ideologies. During the teenage years I became a born-again Christian, focused on a Heavenly Father who I would get to be with again one day, albeit somewhere other than on Earth. In my twenties I worshipped at the feet of a yogic guru, in hopes of achieving enlightenment so that at least after death I would not have to reincarnate on Earth again. In my thirties I joined the Society of Friends (becoming a Quaker), removing the need for an intermediary between myself and God, and finding guidance and inspiration through silent worship in community. I was actively engaged and finding fulfillment in these varied pursuits, but I was also negotiating a profound disconnection between my spirit and my carnal self. I thought, but I struggled to feel. I spoke eloquently, but had little access to the authentic emotions beneath my words. I seem to have obliterated many unpleasant memories.

Experiencing my body as somewhat superfluous, as other than my "real" self, it served my soul as a mere vessel, a temporary home for the part of me that was more eternal, and supposedly more precious. It was as if my soul hovered primarily around and in my head and brain, but was never fully embodied in and as my whole bodily self. It wasn't until my forties, when I grew increasingly unwell, that I became conscious of this disjointed state. Eventually I came to realize that I'd abandoned my bodily self in childhood, something my body had been trying to tell me all along. In living a fast-track, upwardly-mobile professional life, earning academic degrees, seeking career accomplishments, and taking care of my family, I'd been oblivious to my body's signals.

By all accounts my life was a success. I was a professionally accomplished woman, spiritually centered and aware, happily married with wonderful child, living in a lovely home. Yet, something deep inside of me was shutting down. Frightening, sudden panic attacks happened with increasing frequency, interfering with my ability to function. Soon I was at a loss to what I truly felt, and to an authentic sense of myself. In a state of rapid deterioration, it became apparent that my physical health, as well as my emotional and psychological wellbeing, would require that something change. But I didn't know what: I used massage, sand trays, psychotherapy and psychoanalysis, mindfulness practices, crystals and other "grounding" modalities, and prayer, to try to recover a whole and balanced sense of being alive. Eventually I did begin to feel better and to "find my way back home."

It was in my 50s, when I began communicating with horses (as recounted in the book, *When the Horses Whisper*), that the most profound shifts began to occur. That is when the heart center of my body opened, bringing greater awareness of my own and others' feelings. My solar plexus activated, clarifying my core beliefs and heightening my perceptual capacities. My skin sensitized and I discovered what it means to be touched; and my lower chakras bloomed, leading me into amazing expressions of creativity, and a loving, powerful sexuality. Something unexpected was also happening: I was moving from an otherworldly spiritual orientation to directly experiencing the life force in myself, in other people, and in plants and animals. This inner growth, as it turns out, was part of a larger unfolding; gifts have come to me in recent years that have illuminated this often-clouded path.

Part I of *Waking to Beauty* recounts elements of my spiritual journey from early childhood encounters with unseen beings, to the profound sense of interconnectedness that has recently emerged. The content is largely autobiographical in order to provide a contextual framework for the evolution of my intuitive and perceptual abilities. Some of the stories may be mystifying, and possibly alarming, though I don't write with that intention. Rather, my hope is that others will find inspiration and comfort in what's here. When people learn about my ability to communicate with horses, they often ask me whether I have other unusual abilities. They (and I, also for that matter) would like to understand where such a capacity comes from. Is it something one is born with, a "gift" that is revealed at a certain point in life, or perhaps an innate capacity that all human beings have, but one that only some will come to recognize? I do not have an answer to that question. I am, however, able to point to elements of my life journey that may be illuminating.

Part II of *Waking to Beauty* picks up where *When the Horses Whisper* left off, with teachings and lessons I've learned through my continuing communications with horses. The equine species has helped me to sense and hear differently, and to trust what I glean from my body, and from the "still small voice" of intuition from within me. In sharing stories of this, my personal evolution of consciousness, the hope is that others will be encouraged to trust their own unfolding, and to gain the faith and courage they may need as they undergo their own life journeys.

I write this introduction from a porch in Costa Rica, looking out at Arenal, an active andesitic stratovolcano. Plumes of steam are rising from its crater. Through almost two decades of observing this great geological being, including hearing it "breathing" in rhythmic releases of volcanic gas, I have come to see Arenal as a metaphor for humanity. We, too, are made of materials from stars; we, too, receive energy from the depths of Earth, as channels for the uprising flows of the life force.

In *The Desire and Importance of Failing*,[1] the poet Rumi wrote:

"Every part of the cosmos draws toward its mate.
The ground keeps talking to the body,
saying, '*Come back! It's better for you
down here where you came from.*'"

For Rumi this draw represents a conflict between the longing of the soul, and Earth's call. The poem continues,

"We're like four different birds, that each had one leg tied
in with the other birds.
A flopping bouquet of birds!
Death releases the binding, and they fly off,
but before that, their pulling is our pain.
Consider how the soul must be, in the midst of these
tensions, feeling its own exalted pull."

---

[1]Mevlana Jalaluddin Rumi (Mathnawi, III, 4391 – 4472). From "Feeling the Shoulder of the Lion," translated by Coleman Barks

Rumi exhorts us to, "Remember what the soul wants, because in that, eternity is *wanting* our souls!" I know of what he speaks, because for so long I struggled with that "exalted pull" of my soul. Now I question myself, and I question my species, too. Is the pain that is the human condition truly a conflict between the compelling, competing calls of heaven and earth? Perhaps the real problem is in the false dichotomies of our larger belief systems: God as separate from Earth; humans as separate from other animals; spirit as separate from body. In fact, I am beginning to wonder, if we ignore the pull of the earth in its asking us to "come back," in favor of the pull of the soul, what happens to us then? While it is has long been clear to me that our souls live on after bodily death, what matters is that we are alive now. Maybe it is God, or perhaps it is the Tao, but the life force I perceive as in everything and being everywhere, has always been right here with us on Earth.

PART ONE

I Pray the Lord My Soul to Take

RECENTLY I AWOKE FROM a dream, or maybe it wasn't a dream at all. I opened my eyes and saw an intricate, stunningly beautiful pattern of blue and white light above me. It was as if a dome had formed over my head, filled with a shimmering fractal-like pattern. Whispering into the darkness of our bedroom I asked, "What is this?" to which a reply came right away.

> *These are patterns of sound, which normally you cannot see. All sounds take form and every sound creates its own unique pattern. This particular pattern is of the chimes hanging on the porch just outside your window. Their sound has changed the vibrations of your home.*

The knowing voice seemed to be answering from inside me. I considered how different sounds give me different kinds of feelings, the sound of ocean waves versus the sounds of police car sirens, one soothing and the other provoking agitation. As I rose from the bed, moving toward the green glow of the bathroom night-light, it occurred to me that other sounds might not have such pleasant formations. Not long before, I'd been delayed in the Newark airport with thousands of other stranded travelers. I recalled how the cacophony of sounds from multiple announcements of further delays and cancellations, blaring televisions, a roaring carpet cleaner, and people talking, some yelling, turned the concourse into a nerve-wracking environment. "I'd better be careful what I expose myself to," I thought as I shuffled back to bed, imaging the varied patterns of other sounds.

Generally speaking, the human eye does not "see" such vibrations. Nor can it "see" energy. But I have sometimes seen the "unseen." How I have been able to do this I cannot say, other than to surmise that there is a kind of seeing that happens with an apparatus other than the actual physical eyes. A recent example of this was while visiting Costa Rica, I observed a veterinarian as he examined a horse named Amarillo. After the examination Debbie, his caregiver, asked me to check in with Amarillo. In a silent exchange of communication, I asked him how he was feeling, and whether there was anything he wanted the veterinarian to know. Amarillo's response to me came in an image that I could "see" in my mind. It was of hundreds of little tiny, black, worm-like creatures, crawling all over the horse's body. Amarillo said to me, also silently, that he was exhausted from feeling as if he were constantly fighting these creatures. I told Debbie what I'd seen and heard, who then told the veterinarian. His reply was immediate:

"I know exactly what the horse is talking about!" he exclaimed.

The vet reached down to the horse's leg and pulled off a small, black, worm-like parasite. He explained that this was an infestation of the horse's skin, and was something he noticed during the examination.

"This is an easy problem to solve. He needs to be washed with a medicated soap," the vet exclaimed. "After that he'll feel better."

Another example of seeing the unseen is of my son. As an infant lying in his crib, Ari would look up into the corner of his nursery and begin to smile, as if something or someone was there. It is well understood by optometrists that until about three months, a baby's eyes do not focus on objects more than eight to ten inches from their faces. So perhaps what he was seeing was closer than it appeared, or "seen" from another way of seeing. Whatever it was, when he saw it his eyes lit with joyful expression and delight. I'd be looking down into his crib, changing his diaper or changing his clothes, when his eyes would turn looking past me to the object of his attention. I would then turn around in search of what was giving him such delight, but there was never anything there that I could see. Some might surmise this to have been an early indication of the hallucinations Ari would have later in life. But I feel unequivocally that what he was seeing was the being (or beings) that had guided him into this world. It was only there for a few days, and then it was gone.

Similar "seeings" happened for me as a baby. From my mother's telling of it, here's how the story goes:

> One night when Rosalyn was just over a year old, we were visiting my parents in their Philadelphia home, which was not far from where were living. Rosalyn and I were sitting in the living room. I was holding her in my arms when she began to squirm and twitch.
>
> "That's not Butchie, Mommy. That's not Butchie," she said.
>
> Well, Butchie was the man who lived in the apartment above ours, so I assumed that whoever she was seeing looked like him. But I didn't see whom she was talking about.

Closer to Rosalyn's 2ⁿᵈ birthday we were in that same living room at the front of the house. She was playing on the floor near to where I was sitting. Suddenly she looked up, as if responding to the sound of the back door opening. Her body went stiff with fear, and then she lunged into my lap. I watched her as her eyes followed the movement of someone walking from the back of the house, passing through the dining room, and then into the hall and up the stairs. "Who is that boy, Mommy?" she asked me as she watched. Her voice was deep and her tone was serious. The hairs stood up on my arms.

Fortunately for me, when I started exhibiting this propensity my mother was encouraged to read *There is a River* by Thomas Sugrue, the story of Edgar Cayce. As a result, she began to understand me not as the ill child one psychologist had suggested I was, but as someone born with unusual perceptive capacities.

Another story my mother tells is about an event that occurred when I was about three years of age. At that point we were actually living in my grandparents' home. One day I approached my mother who was standing in the kitchen. I said to her, "The lady wants to talk with you."

My mother assumed that someone had come to the front door asking for her, but when she went to the door there was no one there.

"What did the lady look like, Rosalyn?" she asked me, but I had no reply.

When on a second occasion I made reference to "the lady," my mother again asked me to describe her. But I only frowned. Then one day I saw an envelope from my grandmother's church, printed with an artistic representation of The Last Supper. As my mother tells it:

> *Rosalyn looked at the photo excitedly exclaiming, "There's the lady, mommy!" pointing to Jesus who was shown standing at the end of a long table, his hair shoulder-length and brown. He was wearing a white gown so I assumed that the lady Rosalyn was seeing had long hair and was wearing a dress. Then Rosalyn's face grew sad.*
>
> *"Mommy," she exclaimed. "The lady died in a fire."*

In fact, the markings of a fireman's axe suggested there had been a fire in the cellar of that house when Mrs. Scott, the previous owner, occupied it. It was dank, dark, and musty down there. I remember how sometimes sunlight crept through the high window of the small room at the street end of the cellar. That was where coal was delivered through a chute. A wheelbarrow that lay against the wall was used to transport coal to the furnace. The furnace was at the back end of the cellar, near the bottom of the steps. To the eyes of my child self the furnace was a big, dark, cast-iron monster, on four bulky legs, scary unless a protective adult was near. I liked to go down there with my grandfather. I'd perch myself on the steps, about midway down, close enough to watch as my grandfather took hold of the black handle and lifted it, opened the furnace door, and shoveled coal from the barrel, tossing it inside. I was in awe of the blazing inferno. One day while down there, according to my mother, I told my grandfather that the lady was standing at the far end of the cellar. I have no memory of seeing that lady, but I do remember the fright I had over the boy who hovered in the upstairs bedroom of my grandparents' house. I felt terrified when I walked past that room. My mother recalls that I insisted that she watch me whenever I walked down the hallway, from my parent's to my grandparents' bedroom. As she describes it:

> *Rosalyn would walk slowly along the hallway, looking back to be sure I was there. And just before she neared the door to that middle bedroom, she'd bolt past it into the front bedroom. She'd never go alone unless someone was watching.*

On the day we moved out of my grandparent's home I asked, "Mommy, are we going to a *new* house?" She reassured me that we were because we were moving into a newly renovated structure. But according to my mother, a few weeks after we got there I angrily scolded her:

"Mommy, this is NOT a new house!"

I knew this because of the agitated apparition that occupied the empty room between my bedroom and the only bathroom in the apartment. I was frightened to pass there to get into the bathroom, and I never, ever went inside that room. My mother was exacerbated by my fear as she or my father had to get up in the night when I called out, and escort me into the bathroom. Finally, after about two years of our living in that apartment, something changed. I still recall the day I noticed how bright that empty room had become, and I was excited to go in there to explore and to play.

Those were the days when my father would come to say goodnight to my sister and me, and recite with us the bedtime prayer: "Now I lay me down to sleep. I pray the lord my soul to keep. If I should die before I wake. I pray the Lord my soul to take." The prayer ended with "God bless . . ." and a long list of the loved ones who I wanted to be sure would be blessed. My great-grandmother had died when I was about six years old, and I stood by her deceased body, which had been laid on her bed. So I had some sense of what it meant to die. But to do so before waking was a frightful idea at the time.

We moved away from that apartment on Philadelphia's North Franklin Street when I was eight years old, into a stone duplex home on Wayne Avenue, a main artery through the Germantown neighborhood of Philadelphia. It was an historic property, but a quiet one as far as apparitions go. Wayne Avenue was busy day and night with buses, cars, racing police vehicles, alarming ambulances, and electric trolleys that rattled on old steel rails across the cobblestones. On summer nights and weekends, boys bounced basketballs and pushed box carts, navigating the sidewalks of our neighborhood in staking out their territory, while we girls rolled on strap-on skates and played double-dutch, turning the ropes rhythmically, singing. I made friends, but found myself isolated in terms of my inner world, and spent a lot of time alone.

On weekday mornings I walked to Greene Street Friends School. One entered the school through an iron gate, along a slate-covered path, up the stairs of an old stone house, and through its bright red front door. Being a Quaker school, weekly Meeting for Worship was part of our education. During that time the entire student body would assemble, along with our teachers and administrators, to sit in the silence of the historic meetinghouse. My classmates and I would wiggle and squirm and giggle, until we settled in after a few minutes. I remember sitting in Meeting with the genuine hope of hearing or feeling God. That was exactly the point of these gatherings, and if someone were "moved by the spirit" to do so, he or she were to rise to their feet and speak.

Mrs. Franklin was my science teacher at Greene Street Friends. Her teaching left me with two lasting gifts: One is my appreciation for, indeed, my love of "rocks." On our class nature walks with her to the local parks, Mrs. Franklin taught us about the wonderful variety of stones that lay right at our feet. We found mica, white and pink quartz, and also small nuggets of granite, some of which I pocketed and brought home, placing each stone carefully on my windowsill. During one science class Mrs. Franklin happened to mention paranormal phenomena. I approached her privately after lunch that day, as we walked from the dining room back to the classroom building. Excited that maybe she would understand, I shared with her some of the things that were happening to me. Mrs. Franklin listened with openness, as I tried my best to explain how I could "see things." And although she could offer no explanation for what I described, she did offer a willingness to listen, and her empathy was the second of her gifts to me. But there was only so much she could do. I was feeling increasingly isolated, and losing my sense of self. This showed up in "bad girl" behavior such as petty theft, smoking cigars, making small fires, and lying. Then three cats came into our home as pets. The golden tabby that I named Topaz adopted me and his arrival was just in time. Topaz' companionship was my saving grace.

After sixth-grade graduation from Greene Street Friends, I attended an experimental school called "Community Camp School," located on a farm about thirty miles away in Bucks County, Pennsylvania. My most memorable classroom experience from that year was when our science teacher explained the concept of "the environment" in biological terms. It was 1970, and people were beginning to talk about the earth differently; we were part of that "environment" and were responsible for its care. There were horses living on the school property, to one of which I felt a personal connection. When one of the teachers learned of my adoration of horses, she befriended me, and gifted me her ceramic collection of horse figures. These I placed next to my rock collection in the windowsill of my bed-room, along with a miniature orange tree I was growing. In giving the objects the focus of my attention, cherishing them, holding them, and giving them care, I sensed them all but those horses, in particular, took on special aliveness.

One early summer day our family moved again, this time out of state, my sister and I leaving behind grandparents, aunts, uncles, and cousins, in addition to our neighborhood friends. My father, who'd been a music teacher in the Philadelphia pub-lic school system, was heading for a new position, as an assistant professor in Amherst, Massachusetts. My world was suddenly very different. Our New England home, an old, rambling white clapboard farmhouse, was located on a very quiet lane, where the clucks of roosters and moos of cows and an occasional gust of wind across the cornfields offered the only noticeable sounds. To get to school I walked down Pomeroy Lane, to the corner of South Pleasant Street, across from the grassy South Amherst Common, to wait for school bus number 16. Junior high school in Amherst was a cultural shock; for one, I was one of very few African-American students there, and a city girl at that. For two, it was a large, public school, and I'd never been in one of those before.

We rented our home from an octogenarian named Mr. Pomeroy. He was my first introduction to New England cul-ture: terseness, accent and all. It was his family home, and he lived next door in a home built at least a hundred years later than ours. One stipulation on the lease was that the light on the stone pillar at the entrance to the driveway always be turned on. We rarely heard from Mr. Pomeroy unless someone had forgotten this. In which case, he turned the light on himself from a switch wired directly into his house. The pillar had dates inscribed on it from the 1800's, but we were not sure what those dates designated. I was a young teen trying to adjust to a new school and life in a small New England town, a very different world from urban Philadelphia. I wanted to fit in, and to make new friends. The last thing I wanted was to be ostracized for being different. But within a few weeks of our arrival, I began to see and hear apparitions in our rented farmhouse home at 136 Pomeroy Lane.

One was a woman formed of a milky white substance, floating in the hallway upstairs. I didn't like it at all that she was there, because I had to walk right past the apparition to get into my bedroom. No one else saw her, though on a visit with us my grandmother declared that she was awakened by unexplainable noises in the night, coming from the attic. I heard those too; it sounded like a bowling ball rolling back and forth across the attic floor. When my new school friends came to visit for sleepovers, I never mentioned any of this. Two years later our family left that haunted old house, when my parents purchased our own, newly-built house in the center of town. To my relief, and as far as I could tell, we were the only ones in residence there.

How are we to be certain and secure in our individual perceptions, to know what is true, or real, if what we perceive diverts from a shared material reality? What are we to understand about the world, and about ourselves, when the nature and content of our personal experiences reach outside the accepted conventions of knowledge? I suspect, for example, that the "imaginary friends" of some children may actually be companions from the spirit world, like "Joan," who was my sister's playmate, and lived in our home for about two years. In asking my sister Carol as an adult what she remembers about Joan, she cannot say one way or another whether she perceived Joan as imagined or real. She does, however, remember in detail what Joan was like: She had shoulder-length, mousy brown hair with bangs. Her face was pleasant and soft. And she wore a dress. Her complexion and features were suggestive of an Eastern European. She was always located in Carol's bedroom.

Children are given lots of room for the imaginative life, so my guess is that the adults around them thusly categorize such experiences. I have to wonder about people who, like me, as children reveal unusual perceptive capacities. Do they find it difficult to accept their perceptions as real, under the social pressures to adhere to a shared reality? Perhaps many children born with these capacities learn that it's best to shut them down. It seems to me that it would be natural for most people, especially children, to choose the security of "normalcy," and to disregard or suppress "abnormal" perceptions. It must be hard for a child to maintain her natural perceptive capacities when those are out of alignment with those of adults in authority, especially if told repeatedly, "that's just your imagination." Thank goodness, my parents never said that to me.

Sometimes I have felt embarrassment when others learn of my extra-sensory capacities, even though they don't feel "extra" at all. It's just how I experience the world. I recently discussed this with my friend Sally on a visit to Costa Rica, where I often spend time with a herd of therapeutic horses. Sally lives and works in Costa Rica as a horse-led personal development instructor. She offered a helpful reply to my query when I asked her, "Do you think that all people have an innate sixth-sense, or that it is more like a gene that some have and others do not?"

Sally explained that to her way of thinking, the human species had it and used it earlier in its evolution, but lost it largely when language was acquired. But some of us never lost it entirely. More and more, Sally believes, many people are redis-covering that part of themselves, and horses can assist with that because they never lost this capability. That makes sense to me, and explains a lot. Though I have to accept that some things do not yet have explanations. Like what happened when in high school I took a trip to New York City.

My father was driving to New York City to work on a proj-ect with a fellow musician. My friend Sabra and I decided to go along, as there was an extra guest room we could stay in. It was the mid-1970s and New York was not the place it is today it terms of safety or cleanliness. We were young, fearless, and adventuresome and explored the city on our own, with no sense of danger. My grandmother had given me her full-length white rabbit fur coat. In my complete oblivion to the attraction it would be, I wore that coat on our night out. Walking along the streets of mid-town Manhattan, not far from the theater district, we turned down a very quiet, dimly-lit side street, with no appar-ent commercial establishments. Suddenly, a man crossed the street and approached us. When about seven feet away he slipped his hand into his jacket and pulled out a pair of numchucks, a wooded-handled weapon used in martial arts. Sabra and I locked arms as the man raised his weapon: but in a flash, Sabra and I were suddenly across the street and turning onto 8th Avenue.

A few hours later, laying on our respective twin beds, in the darkness of the guest room of my father's colleague, we shared our relief and horror over the situation. And we searched unsuccessfully for an explanation of how we got out of harm's way. Even after these many years, Sabra and I still wonder what happened, and ponder the possibilities of what might have protected us from what we both perceived to be an impending attack. Was it a presence we could not see that came to our aid, or could we perhaps for a moment, have stepped outside of three-dimensional reality?

The next summer, between my sophomore and junior year of high school, my sister and I were sent to Chop Point, a Christian summer camp in Maine. It was a loving community and we had a wonderful time. The activities were great, including sailing, tennis, and snorkeling. And the food was amazing: fresh fish, fresh vegetables, and homemade bread and pies. We were very well cared for there. I became more focused on the religious aspects of camp than did my sister, whose primary interest and passion was the athletics. I attended and often led the sunrise prayer sessions at "Meditation Rock," and participated in the optional bible study in the evenings.

My parents were not religious and did not attend church, though both my maternal and paternal grandparents were very active churchgoers. Back when we lived in Philadelphia, I'd sometimes accompany my grandmother to her church. I fondly remember sitting in the pew by her side, taking communion with her, singing hymns from the hymnal we shared. During the sermons, which I was too young to follow, I stared with great interest at the stained glass art that filled the windows of the First Presbyterian church on Venango Street. When we moved into our own home in Germantown, and I was old enough to venture out on my own, I attended random churches alone that I could walk to in my neighborhood. This is all to say that even at a very young age, I yearned for something that religions seemed to offer.

At summer camp, we were encouraged to memorize the verses of Isaiah 53, and to recite the Lord's Prayer from the book of Matthew, in the New Testament Christian bible. I had already learned this prayer from attending services with my grandmother, and from my father, who somewhere along the way had replaced the "now I lay me down to sleep," with this one:

"Our Father, who art in heaven, hallowed be thy name.
Thy kingdom come, thy will be done,
on Earth as it is in heaven.
Give us this day our daily bread.
And forgive us our trespasses, as we
forgive those who trespass against us.
And lead us not into temptation but deliver us from evil.
For thine is the kingdom, and the power,
and the glory forever. Amen."

I wanted so much to be righteous, accepted by the camp community and by God, or at least by that which I understood God to be through the camp's teachings. I tried to convince myself that I understood what and where heaven was, as God's abode, and to conceive such a kingdom as was coming. Motivated by the counselors and my peers in that Christian community, and feeling that I had found God, I rendered my testimony and was born again.

With the regular bible study and daily prayers, I became inspired by a sense of community, and of God's love for me. I went with other campers into the streets of Bath, Maine to witness my faith, proclaiming how in Christ my life had changed.

But when I returned the following summer as a counselor in training, and shared stories of my experiences with the spirit world, the other camp counselors suggested that these were of an occult nature and certainly not of God. I was told that having been born again, and having accepted Jesus as my personal savior, such encounters with the spirit world would stop. But when the summer ended and I returned home, the paranormal experiences returned. I was still devoted, reading the bible and praying morning and night. I had just turned eighteen years old and believed I had "been saved." They'd spoken about "the devil" at camp. And I believed what they taught, about his power to affect our lives in negative ways. But if the influence of "the devil" explained the spirit world that I continued to perceive, then what did that mean about me?

At that time we had a dog we named Laddie, a very smart full-blooded Beagle. When Laddie came into the house from his romps outdoors, I always knew he was back because I could hear his nails making a pitter-patter sound against the wooden floor above my bedroom. Tragically, Laddie became the victim of overzealous play by a neighbor's dog when their play got rough; Laddie was bitten in his throat, and bled profusely. The veterinarian did what he could but our beloved Laddie died on his table. A few days later, I began to hear that same pitter patter sound of Laddie's nails, moving back and forth along the upstairs hallway. Our happy dog had come back home, though it was his spirit that returned.

During that fall, my senior year of high school, my boyfriend's parents moved out of their large, historic home to a beachside town on Cape Cod. The home they left was empty but still accessible, so on the last weekend before Scott would be moving away to join his family, we decided to spend the night there. We'd gone first to a party, which ran until well after midnight; it was late and we were tired by the time we arrived at the house. It was quite dark inside because the electric service had been turned off. This was a large home of at least 5,000 square feet, built in 1895. It had wooden floors and tall ceilings, and was emptied of rugs, draperies, and furniture, so the acoustics made our voices echo. As we climbed the steps to the second floor, I stopped on the landing to sing a few lines of a favorite song. We then managed to find our way in the dark up to Scott's former bedroom at the back on the house. This is where he wanted to spend his last night in his hometown. We put our sleeping bags down on the bare floor and climbed inside them. It was just after 1:00 a.m. and Scott quickly fell asleep. But I did not because of the sound of a soprano's singing.

"Are you hearing that?" I asked Scott, waking him. The haunting voice was inside the home and seemed to be coming from a nearby room.

"Hearing what?" he replied.

"That woman singing. Don't you hear her?"

"Must be the ghost," he mumbled, turning away to fall back asleep.

Later that night, in need of the bathroom, I was anxious about going alone for fear that I might encounter that spirit. The boundary between one dimension and another, between that of spirit and matter had been blurred for me. Although the singing had stopped, I knew she was probably still somewhere in that house at 151 Amity Street. If I could see and hear her, might she also be able to see and hear me? I lay there for a while until finally I pushed past the fear.

"I was born this way," I thought as I climbed out of my sleeping bag and moved as quickly as I could down the hall and into the bathroom. I reminded myself of how the other times I'd encountered a ghost I had come to no harm. I returned to Scott's bedroom, my bladder relieved, but even more relieved that I'd not seen the singing woman.

Not wanting to accept what I had been told at the Christian summer camp, that my perceptual abilities were of evil influence, I sought another kind of God in which to believe. But in being young, eager, and open to many possibilities, I was vulnerable in my searching.

While passing through the Campus Center of the University of Massachusetts one day, I was drawn to a table with a placard that read, "Holy Spirit Association for the Unification of World Christianity."

"What a wonderful idea!" I thought.

"What's this about?" I asked the two people who were sitting behind the long table.

"We're with the Unified Family," one of them explained.

"Who's that person?" I inquired; looking at a photo captioned "Reverend Sun Myung Moon." They explained that he was the founder of their movement. Moon taught that God is the creator and our heavenly parent, being both feminine and masculine by nature, and whose center is true love. That sounded good to me. So I agree to attend an informational dinner the next night in their home. When I arrived I was taken upstairs to a room, where they turned off the lights and left me to watch a film of Moon speaking. Completely bored, I dozed through the film, and my hosts were annoyed about that. Afterwards they fed me a spaghetti meal, and asked what questions I had. I couldn't come up with any, which seemed to annoy them even more. The couple struck me as strange, sort of lethargic in their demeanor; but my interest remained so when they invited me to attend a weekend retreat I said, "Sure." On the night before said retreat, I was out late socializing with my friends. When the woman arrived at my home early in the morning to pick me up, I was still asleep. My mother answered the door. I stirred when the doorbell rang, but I did not awake fully enough to hear their exchange. My mother came to tell me that she had sent away a "bedraggled" woman who was here to pick me up for the weekend. My mother wanted an explanation and I had none; I was naïve.

Soon thereafter we learned of "kidnappings" and subsequent "brainwashing" that had occurred to people who were taken on weekend retreats by "the Moonies" (as they came to be called by the media). I'd been spared, and at least for a short while, abandoned my search for a religion or "truth" that would provide if not a full explanation, at least a measure of tolerance for my unusual perceptual capacities. Until, that is, the day I came from school shaken, and broke into tears when my mother greeted me. All these years later, she still clearly remembers that day and recounts from her memory my response when she asked me, "Rosalyn, what's wrong?"

"Last night I dreamed everything that happened today. All day it was like watching a movie I'd already seen. This is scaring me."

II

Om Namah Shivaya

IN HIGH SCHOOL I was a student leader and actively involved in our small New England college town. But in terms of academics I was more social than studious. Until, that is, I befriended a group of debate team members who were serious honor roll students, and very smart. Being around them motivated me: I put my mind to my studies and did well; enough to convince my teachers and myself that I was a great and capable student. So when it was time to apply for college I did as my friends did, and submitted applications for admission to the likes of Harvard, Wellesley, Brown, Bucknell, Bates, and Duke. My mother, a university admissions counselor at the time, had tried to warn me that my choices were unrealistic. But I didn't listen. On April 15th, the arrival day of admission decisions, I came home from school to find an unopened pile of letters stacked on the dining room table. With some slight variation each of them contained the words, "Dear Miss Wiggins: After careful review by the admissions committee, we regret to inform you that your application has been denied . . ."

I was stunned, and had no idea what to do. My practical mother handed me the Peterson's Guide to colleges, a heavy

500-page paperback—there was no Internet and no personal computers—and she told me how to search out the schools that had rolling or late application deadlines, and also the financial aid I would need. Finally in midsummer I heard from Hampton Institute in Virginia with an offer for admission. I enrolled and early that September, I moved south into what was an alien culture for me. Academically, I excelled as a college freshman, and won competitions on the forensics (public speaking) team. When I decided that I wanted to major in speech communications, my coach said, "You should go to UVA." I'd never heard of the place so I wasn't particularly interested. But she persisted and was encouraging, so I applied. I braced for the rejection, and to my surprise, was offered admission and a scholarship.

That fall I stepped sight unseen into yet another unfamiliar world, nothing like inner city Philadelphia, or the small town of Amherst, Massachusetts, or even Hampton Institute in the same state. There I was attending a traditional southern university in 1976, dressed in an imported maxi-skirt and tie-dyed tee, with a sandalwood mala (Hindu prayer beads) hanging from my neck. While my fellow female students wore khaki knee-length skirts, button-up argyle sweaters draped over their shoulders, a string of pearls or gold add-a-beads around their necks. And the guys mostly wore blue blazers and collared shirts, some even with ties, khaki pants, and either Docksiders or shiny loafers. And there were fraternities and sororities with their own houses that threw keg parties with live rock bands on weekends. Bluegrass music played at night on our college radio station. My father was a jazz musician, and my mother favored classical music. I'd been exposed to those genres, and the pop, folk, and soul music of my teenage years, but knew nothing of bluegrass. I quickly grew to appreciate its lively combination of fiddle and banjo, and hearing it made me feel good.

In October of fall semester I went to watch a hypnotist perform. The hypnotist called on those in the audience who were willing to take the stage and be hypnotized. About twenty-five of us were selected from the slew of raised hands, though it hadn't occurred to me when I volunteered that we would become the entertainment! After determining who among us would be hypnotizable, he sent over half of that group back to their seats. If I recall correctly, about ten remained on stage, including me. I went under hypnosis quickly and deeply, following the instructions he gave. When the hypnotist suggested that I was a ballet dancer, I imagined myself as graceful and adept, while clumsily leaping across the stage. The audience broke into uproarious laughter. The hypnotist then told the man standing next to me that I stank like nothing he'd ever smelled, and when that man's face formed into a disgusted glare at me; again, the audience roared.

After the show I left the theater alone, walking home to the university housing complex where I lived. I can still remember the autumn night air on my face as I walked, my feeling weightlessness as if floating above the ground, and having no sense of time. Everything around me seemed to be charged with an energetic aliveness.

Shortly after I got back there was a knock on the door to my apartment. I opened it to find my friend Chris standing there. He'd been at the show and seen me on stage, and was full of excitement about the evening. Still feeling serene, and in an altered state consciousness, I invited Chris to have a seat on the couch. I don't know why I did what I did next, but I took his hand into mine and closed my eyes. An image formed in my mind. It was of a woman with curly brown hair, standing behind a white picket fence in the front yard of a brick Cape Cod-style home. When I described what I saw to Chris, he lurched, snatching his hand away from mine.

"That's my house!" he declared standing up. "And my mother, too! How do you know what she looks like?"

At the time I did not have an answer for Chris, and I'm not sure I have one now. Maybe the visual information I received came directly from Chris, who though unaware was carrying images in his consciousness and making those available to me. I don't think that I "read" his mind in some privately invasive way. (Even if it were possible, that would be inappropriate.) Maybe what happened is that I tuned into a mental vibration of sorts, or a field of consciousness emitted by my friend. Whatever the reason for the unusual occurrence, it probably happened because the hypnosis left me in a particularly receptive state.

Now I was to be seen as someone different, even spooky. But I managed to make other friends, and in continuing to adjust to this new culture, joined the International Club and the competitive forensics team. For my work-study job, and to help with my expenses, I transcribed the papers of George Washington, taught swimming classes in the university pool, babysat, and waited tables in a downtown restaurant. After weekday classes and on Sundays, I'd study in the reference room of the university library. Sometimes, just out of curiosity, I'd explore the narrow rows of the dimly-lit old stacks, pulling random books off of the shelves, and then sit on the floor to thumb through them. That's how I first discovered works of mysticism such as *The Cloud of Unknowing*, anonymously authored, written in the latter half of the 14th century. For study breaks I read that, and other similar works of mysticism.

It was not long before I felt the pull back into a spiritual life. In a small, three-line classified listing of the local newspaper, I discovered a community called Unity. They were meeting in the conference room of The Boar's Head Inn, a local hotel located about two miles west of the university. Once again, I was drawn to the word "unity" because the meaning it evoked for me was union with God, and that's exactly what I'd wanted. I assumed this would be different from the "Unified Family" organization I'd encountered before. So I left a message of inquiry on the phone line that was given in the newspaper listing, and was heartened to receive a return call from a member of the church, who offered to give me a ride from my dormitory to the Sunday services.

I attended Unity Church regularly, the only young person among a group of about twenty older adults. It was wonderful. In that particular religious community, I was reassured that I was not a sinner who'd strayed into the devil's territory, but rather, a person who'd been born with the capacity to see and feel into other realities. This was a Christianity that focused on the positive, and what they called "practical Christianity," based on principles of truth that promoted health, prosperity, happiness, and peace of mind. I felt at home there, accepted just the way I was. I especially enjoyed the minister's guided meditations, through which I was able to feel a sense of peace in myself, and a restored sense of connection with God. And the affirmations we recited became part of my daily prayers. Especially this one:

"The Light of God Surrounds me.
The love of God unfolds me.
The power of God protects me.

The presence of God watches over me.
Wherever I am, God is. And where God is, all is well."

It seemed that I had found my spiritual home, so much so that during the fall of the next academic year, my junior year of college, I asked our beloved minister how I might become a Unity minister myself. Sadly, his counsel for me was to pursue other careers, explaining that at that time, the Missouri-based seminary would not be welcoming to someone of my race. Within a few months I found myself at the local Quaker meeting on Sunday mornings, practicing silent worship without a minster, as was familiar from my childhood Quaker schooling.

When springtime came I began dating a man named Alexis. One night that June, with him in Virginia and me in Massachusetts, I heard Alexis speaking to me while I was falling asleep. But his words were not audible in the normal way and didn't come from inside of my bedroom or in the house. It was coming from very far away, heard through inner sounds saying, "I can't be with you anymore."

A few days later Alexis called me on the telephone to say that very same thing. I shared with him that I already knew he was breaking up with me, and therefore I was prepared. After I explained to him how I knew, Alexis told me that on the same night and at precisely the same time I'd heard him, he had gone out into the pasture by his grandmother's house in rural Buckingham County, Virginia, looked up at the stars and shouted at the top of his voice, "I can't be with you anymore, Rosalyn!"

That same summer, between my sophomore and junior year of college, I began to have another kind of experience I could not explain. At night, as I was falling asleep, I'd feel a vibration in my feet, which would move up though my entire body and then out of my head. The first time this happened, I found that my perspective went from lying on my bed looking up, to staring down at my body lying on my bed from up at the ceiling, I assumed it was a dream. Except that it continued to happen, and on subsequent occasions it seemed that I was moving around the house, and going outside, before re-entering my body. Once, as I remember it, the vibrations came and suddenly I was moving up into the night sky, and then moving through the darkness over New York City. I descended to the street, in front of a brownstone building, climbed its exterior steps and walked through its front door, up an interior staircase, to a landing on the second floor. A woman came to the door and I spoke with her, and then returned home, to my body and bed.

About two weeks later, I was actually in New York City, there with friends for a weekend of museums and other entertainment. I was driving around in a residential area on the upper West side of the city, in search of a place to eat. My travelling companions were startled when I suddenly put on the brakes. I was startled, too. We were in front of the very same brownstone house I'd visited during my out-of-body travels, a building I'd never seen before. I pulled into a parking space, and walked up the steps to discover the front door was unlocked. It was an apartment building. I opened the door and found the same interior staircase I'd climbed in an altered state of awareness, just as I'd remembered it; it had not been a dream. But rather than try to find the woman I'd spoken with while in that out-of-body state, I turned around and left.

Without any conscious intention on my part, these travels out of body became more regular that summer, until one horrid occasion I returned to my bedroom to discover there were milky white, gremlin-like beings, clamoring over my sleeping body. A battle ensured, with me screaming at them to get away. I slipped back into my body self and then put forth a prayer, asking God to keep me from ever leaving again, at least until my death. But I also wondered, was it up to me, or would God intervene and protect me? From this frightening encounter I began to question the nature of reality, and the existence of an active and at times unruly spirit world that lies beyond the view of most of us, one that can be fraught with danger if we are not careful. I sought refuge from that world, in the safety of shared reality in the material realm. But I also endeavored to better understand.

When I returned to college after that summer, for my third year of undergraduate studies, I walked off campus down Main Street in Charlottesville, in search of a spiritual bookstore I'd heard about. I explained to the store clerk what had been happening to me. She introduced herself as Kay, the owner of Quest Books. Coming out from behind the counter, she led me to the shelf to find Robert Monroe's *Journeys Out of the Body*. The book had been published in 1971, seven years before. In reading it I learned about the existence of an astral body, as an energetic-spirit form of the individual bodily self, which can leave the physical body at will. What I did not glean from the reading was why I was doing this, since I had neither intended nor desired such experiences. I certainly was not doing it on purpose.

That was nearly forty years ago, and I have no knowledge of leaving my body since then, except very recently when I was visiting an out-of-town friend. While I was asleep in her guest room in the middle of the night, the bedroom door opened and a naked man walked in. Sometimes when I talk in my sleep, I can hear myself speaking without fully waking; on this occasion I was aware of myself anxiously telling this person to get out. But he instead climbed into the bed and lay down beside me. I then recognized this man as my host, and friend's husband. He made overtures to engage me sexually, and I became angry. Despite my efforts to physically push him away, he persisted. I looked at him sternly saying, "I really don't want you here. I am devoted to my husband and have no intentions of having sex with you." On hearing that, he rose from the bed and left the room.

I stirred enough to realize what had just happened, and awoke fully, surmising that the entire episode had happened outside of the material realm, or else was of a different energetic vibration than the usual personal encounter. He seemed to be entirely out of his physical body, and I near but not entirely inside of mine. The next morning when my friend's husband greeted me with a warm friendly smile, it was apparent that he had no awareness of what had happened the night before. How many people, I wonder, leave their bodies during sleep, travelling with no realization of doing so?

During my junior year in college and again shortly thereafter, I experienced the life force vibration in another, more comfortable way. My maternal grandmother, who we affectionately referred to as "Mom-Mom," was suffering from end-stage colon cancer. By my second semester of studies that year, the disease had advanced beyond treatment. In March she was moved from a hospital in Philadelphia to my parent's home in Amherst, Massachusetts, and within a few weeks she was receiving hospice care there. I was very close to my grandmother. I wanted to be by her side in her final days, but I was 500 miles away at school, had no car, nor did my parents have the money for me to fly or to take the train home. Besides, with final exams approaching I knew my grandmother would want me to stay at school and focus on my studies. A few times over the weeks of her staying with my parents, my mother would sometimes call and put my grandmother's ear to the phone. In that way I was able to speak to her. But as for regular contact, it just didn't happen. I was studying, she was dying, and there was nothing else I could do.

Early one Sunday morning in late April, while taking a hot shower, I began to experience an odd sensation of vibrations in my body. Beginning in my feet they moved upward, from my lower legs into my thighs, through my pelvis, abdomen, chest, and throat, and finally out through the top of my head. It happened in a matter of seconds. While this sensation was like the approach of my earlier out-of-body travel, I stayed in my body.

"What is going on?" I thought, perplexed. I turned off the faucet, drew back the shower curtain, and stepped onto the bathmat to try to get a better sense of it. But the vibrations had stopped and were not repeated. Wrapping myself in a towel I sat down on the tub's edge, wondering what to make of the occurrence. That's when the telephone rang. No one else was in the apartment at the time, and so it was up to me to answer the phone. I scurried down the hall into the common room where the phone was.

"Hello?" I said.

My mother's voice was low and somber.

"Mom—Mom just died."

I numbed myself to the shock, put grieving on hold, and finished the semester's courses and exams. It was another two weeks before I broke down, realizing the finality of her death: I would never again melt into my grandmother's gentle embrace; see her round, brown eyes smiling at me; smell the scent of perfume on her neck; feel the softness of her powdered cheek against mine; share a hymnal and sing, sitting by her side in a pew of her church; or eat her homemade fried chicken and candied yams. I would miss her terribly. But as I came to discover (and will explain shortly), my grandmother was deceased but she was certainly not gone.

As I settled into my parents' home for the summer back in Amherst, her absence was palpable. One evening in late July, in the midst of a family meal, an anxious feeling came that led me to go outside. I sat down on the front steps, alone in the dark, soothed by the rhythm of chirping crickets and the cool New England air. That's when that same undulating energy began: the vibrations started in my feet, then coursed upward through my body, and finally out the top of my head. I gazed up at the stars and a deep sense of calm came over me. A few minutes later, my father opened the front door. A call had come in from New Jersey. The news was unexpected. My paternal grandfather had just died. I would miss him, too.

It's apparent that the vibrations I felt moving through and out of my body happened at the same time that my maternal grandmother and paternal grandfather were dying. This leads me to believe that even beyond genetics, their bodies were connected to mine, and that because of my sensitivities I was able to feel it directly when they passed away. It's not far from this idea to the possibility that being alive involves an encompassing energy, which leaves the body at the time of death but continues to exist. (This could certainly be one explanation for my encounters with people who are deceased.) What's curious and less apparent to me is how this energy is shared, connecting us to one another through time and space.

I returned to college that September for my final year of undergraduate studies, and moved into an apartment with Gordon, my boyfriend and future husband. One night, shortly after we had fallen asleep, I sensed something hovering above our bed, causing me to wake up. I knew that it was my grandmother, because I felt the same as I did in her presence when she was alive. In unspoken words, we communicated: she'd come because she wanted to know what Gordon was like. I told her that I was happy that she had come, since I truly loved this man, and one of my disappointments on her dying was that they'd never met. Then she made a stunning request:

"May I come back through you?"

Could she have been asking to be born again as my child?

I'd learned about reincarnation in Hinduism classes. I was aware of the burgeoning research on the subject being done by Dr. Ian Stevenson at the University of Virginia. Conceptually, it made sense to me that if we are spirit beings composed of an ethereal kind of energy (and energy cannot be destroyed, only changed) then why would we not continually re-enter materiality, taking form as another living being? My grandmother was a devout Christian, and she never spoke of such things in her life. Yet this is what she seemed to be speaking of in her visit with me that evening.

"Yes, of course!" I told her through the silent, inner voice that I used to communicate across the boundaries of physicality.

She left and I fell into a deep and peaceful sleep.

After I graduated from college in 1979 and returned to Massachusetts, my godmother invited me to join her for a weekend retreat. She wanted me to meet Swami Muktananda, her guru. I'd never heard of Siddha Yoga, and knew nothing about the guru-disciple relationship. But I adored and respected my godmother, so I accepted the invitation and met her there. The retreat was held in a very large hotel complex of the Catskills in New York State, formerly a property offering entertainment and summer getaways for New York's Jewish community. It had been totally transformed, with images of Hindu gods and goddesses on the walls, the scent of Nag Champa incense wafting through the corridors, and a huge auditorium turned meditation hall. The meals were entirely vegetarian offerings of dal, and rice, and curried vegetables, cooked by "ashram-ers" in residence as volunteers, self-served and eaten family style in large dining halls. I sat with the four hundred or so women on the left side of the hall, while another three hundred or so men sat on the right. When the guru entered the meditation hall, a hush came over the entire room. Adorned in the classic red silk garments of a monk, Muktananda passed us in silence, then took his seat on the raised guru's throne. I listened to him, enraptured, as he explained the meaning of the mantra Om Namah Shivaya. Shiva is the Hindu god of destruction, who destroys the ego mind state that keeps us from perceiving our true state as one with God. In repeating that particular mantra we are bowing to the presence of Shiva (a.k.a. Siva), honoring God as present within us. When the time came for my personal initiation, Muktananda's hands pressing my forehead and his peacock feathers hitting my head, I soared into a sense of immense expansiveness, and utter stillness. I'd felt something I'd never experienced, as if the entire universe was inside of me.

For the next ten years I returned to the ashram, prostrating before the guru and sitting "at his feet." Dutiful and enthralled, I listened to his teachings, practiced the meditation techniques he taught, repeated the mantras he gave, and participated in the daily, hour-long ritual of chanting 128 verses of the Gurugita (the Guru's song). This ancient text describes a conversation between Lord Shiva and his wife the Goddess Parvati, in which she is taught about the guru, and the guru's capacity to instill liberation in the devoted seeker. The root "gu" stands for darkness, and "ru" for light. In his capacity to remove such darkness, the Guru is said to reveal the light of the heart.

After my initiation into Siddha Yoga and with the subsequent practices, I experienced dramatic movements of Kundalini, the primal energy located at the base of the spine. Bodily shaking, random vocalizations of animal and other sounds, visions of swirling energy and blue lights, were among the experiences these practices brought on. The most dramatic movements always occurred after Muktananda delivered Shaktipat or aktip ta (from the Sanskrit shakti "(psychic) energy" and p ta, "to fall") the conferring of spiritual "energy" upon one person by another. Indeed, as intended, practicing this spiritual path had "touched and expanded my inner mystical state." I hoped and believed that if I continued my meditation and chanting practices, it would be just a matter of time until I'd be "established in my experience of oneness with God."

The next winter, having enrolled in a graduate student program, I spent a semester abroad in India. Our program began in the city of New Delhi, where our student group took day trips to places of historic and architectural significance, like the Taj Mahal and the Red Fort. One morning while I was eating breakfast by the window of the hotel dining room, I observed our chartered bus arrive and my fellow students climbing on. I was flustered and confused; somehow I missed the announcement of a trip. I scurried out and joined the group, unaware of our destination. As we rode along the narrow streets of Old Delhi, the intricate, historic architecture captured my attention. Then onto a modern boulevard we drove until stopping at what looked like a manicured garden park. Everyone got off of the bus and proceeded through the gates of the site. My classmates wandered off to explore, while I elected to walk with our professor, Dr. Rao.

"Where are we?" I asked him, feeling curiously peaceful, and sensing we were in hallowed territory.

"This is Raj Ghat, a memorial to Mahatma Gandhi," he returned in his soft-spoken voice.

During my undergraduate studies I'd taken Dr. Rao's course on Gandhi philosophy. We'd learned that Gandhi was shot on the way to a prayer meeting, and that before losing consciousness he made the Hindu gesture of forgiveness.

"This is the site of Gandhi's cremation," Dr. Rao explained as we arrived at the flower-covered marble monument. Together we stood silently, in reverence.

After a week in New Delhi we travelled by plane to Mysore, a city in the Karnataka province of southern India. The air there was fragrant with spices and flowers, cow dung, and exhaust from the diesel-powered trains. By the second day I was wearing a silk sari, with bangles on my ankles and wrists, and the red mark of a bindi right between my brows. We spent the remainder of our semester in Mysore, residing in dormitories on the campus of a local food science college. For breakfast we drank sweet, milky black tea and ate warm dal with fresh-made chapattis rolled up into delicious tubes. To get to classes we rode our bikes past mango stands and barefoot children carrying cement blocks onto construction sites. I made new friends of local college students; Hindus, Muslims, women and men, of Tanzanian exchange students, and the merchants who sold me fresh-made mango lassis after class.

We attended classes inside the famous Palace of Mysore, where Dr. Rao taught us about the Yoga Sutras, the Bhagavad-Gita, and the Upanishads, which are sacred texts of Hinduism.

I continued with my daily Siddha Yoga meditation and chanting practices.

Sometime towards the end of our semester, an excursion to a Tibetan Buddhist refugee camp was arranged for the group. Late during the night before we were to go, in a state somewhere between asleep and awake, I heard the sound of a man's voice. It was saying, "Don't go tomorrow." Although the voice seemed to be coming from inside my dormitory room, I could not fathom how that was possible. It was a very small room, about ten feet by eight, holding only a twin bed, a dresser, and a desk. I had no roommate and was there alone.

Groggy, I sat upright in the dark and listened. Surmising the voice to have been only a dream, I lay back down and closed my eyes, aiming to fall back asleep.

"Don't go tomorrow," I heard once more.

I sat up again, wide-awake this time. I reached my hand under the mosquito netting that was tented over my bed. There were often power outages so I kept a flashlight on the nightstand. I picked it up, turned it on, and scanned the dormitory room.

"Is someone here?" I whispered, pointing the light beam at the open closet, under the desk, and at the door. I even peeked under my bed. No one was anywhere in the room that I could see, and no one replied to my inquiry. I turned off the flashlight, lay down again, and pulled the sheet up close to my neck. Intending to disregard what I thought I'd heard, I attempted to go back to sleep. Instead I lay there awake, listening in the darkness.

"Don't go tomorrow," the voice repeated for the third time.

"Okay! I won't go," I yelled, pulling the sheet over my head. Shortly thereafter I fell asleep.

Early the following morning my classmates and Dr. Rao gathered outside of the dormitory to wait for the hired cars.

Not wanting to cause a stir, I came out to join them and quietly explained to Dr. Rao about the message I had received in the night. I'd decided to remain behind that day. He nodded in understanding and bid me a good day. But my fellow students were bewildered when I turned back towards the dormitory.

"Why aren't you coming with us?" one called out. I didn't know what to say.

Watching from my dormitory window as the caravan of cars drove off with my classmates and professor, I felt sadly disappointed. I'd truly been excited about the trip. Later that evening the group returned, all except for three people. Apparently students had packed themselves tightly inside the cars, piled on each other's laps, and without wearing seatbelts. One car had been rolled off the road and ended up in a ditch. Its driver and passengers had gone to a hospital. They'd incurred a few scratches and bumps, and one student had a mild concussion. I don't speculate about my decision to stay behind and what might have happened had I gone along. All I know is that I'd heard what I heard, and trusted it. And when something similar happened about ten years later, I took heed again.

It happened about five years after marrying Gordon, my college sweetheart. Our first pregnancy ended in a spontaneous miscarriage at about three week's gestation. I was ignorant of such things, and completely shocked when I saw what had fallen into the toilet on the day I had such bad cramps. Home alone, I sat up on the edge of my bed and cried inconsolably, not understanding how could this have happened, or why? Then I felt my great-grandmother Lummie Lee, moving towards me. Her form was very faint. I had not seen her since 1963, when I was only four years old; on the day my mother led me to the bedside where her corpse was laid. The crying stopped as I sensed her hand reaching for mine. She'd come to comfort me and I knew then that it would be okay.

We waited about six months before trying again. The second pregnancy had gone full term, and we were two weeks away from the due date. I woke up one morning without a precise memory, yet knowing that I'd dreamt about the pregnancy and that something was wrong. I called the obstetrician's office right away. They scheduled an appointment for that afternoon.

"I want you to do an internal exam," I insisted.

As I sat on the examination table the doctor explained that an internal exam is not standard protocol at thirty-eight weeks gestation. He reassured me that I was probably just anxious, this being my first full-term pregnancy. But I pressed him until he finally agreed. Lying on my back, feet in the stirrups, I tried to remain calm when he said, "I can't feel the baby's skull."

They arranged for an ultrasound appointment an hour later across town at the university hospital. I drove there directly from the obstetrician's office and my husband met me there. We were immediately taken into the examination room. The sonographer followed the normal routine, but when he couldn't find what he was looking for he called in the radiologist. She stared at the screen, took the instrument into her own hands, added more jelly to my abdomen and began searching for herself. Then she said something I'd never expected to hear:

"We need to get an x-ray, right away."

I knew enough to know that x-rays are not routine for a pregnancy. Something was definitely wrong.

Gordon and I sat in ignorance as we waited for the results. I pondered the dream I'd had the night before, which began this chain of events. Had it been my internal knowing, and my own subconscious warning to me? It was just after 5:00 p.m. when the radiologist came back in to speak with us. Office hours were over, but she told us that our obstetrician would wait in his office for us to return. We were to go there immediately.

I cursed the traffic that slowed my drive back downtown, my breathing shallow and my blood pressure elevated. When Gordon and I walked through the front door and into the obstetrician's office waiting room Eileen the nurse was standing there. She could not hide her mournful expression so in that way, we had been forewarned. We were led into the doctor's office where he sat somberly behind his desk. The fetus' condition was anencephaly, "without a brain," which is always fatal since it's the brain that keeps the baby alive after being disconnected from the mother's life-supporting umbilicus.

When we got home I called my parents to apologize. They'd been so excited about the upcoming birth of their first grandchild. My father wouldn't accept my apology. Rather, he asked, "Since when do you control the molecules of the universe?"

I'd not yet begun to learn that lesson. I still thought that my own choices and actions, even my will, could have tremendous influence over my life. I'd done everything the pregnancy guidebooks said to do, and in addition had taken a super-high-potency vitamin-food supplement pill made just for pregnancy. I suspected this had been the cause of my daughter's fatal abnormality, as the levels of B complex in that pill were 3,000 times the recommended daily amount. I believed that by error in judgment I might have been to blame for her missing brain. Something had to be done to ameliorate this tragedy.

Over the next two weeks I tried to arrange for our child's organs to be donated, given her imminent death. I didn't know what else to do with myself while waiting for her to be born, or how to correct for my irresponsible choices. I wanted to make a horrid situation less so by helping another child to live.

Two weeks later, at the due date, there was still no softening or dilation of my cervix. Without the pressure of a hardened fetal skull the cervix didn't receive the input for the hormones to respond. The obstetrician induced labor. It was a very long process, beginning in the evening with the insertion of seaweed sticks, a procedure that ultimately failed. The next morning they put an IV into my arm and a Pitocin drip was begun, which finally led to a mild onset of labor. I labored all through the morning and into the afternoon, when I slipped into a semi-conscious state. The attending nurses and my husband all witnessed it when at about 2:25 p.m., I opened my eyes and announced, "The baby will be born at 3:12 p.m."

But 3:12 p.m. came and went and I continued to labor. At 5:00 p.m. the obstetrician instructed me, "Push harder."

I pushed, and pushed, and pushed until she finally crowned. The doctor rolled back his stool and folded his arms across his chest. The room took on the atmosphere of a wake: faces somber, eyes down, a completely silent crowd of medical personnel standing by, some of whom were there to assist the doctor, others who were there to whisk the baby away at birth, as part of the protocol for the pre-arranged organ transplantation process. A few people were peeking in from the hallway as curious onlookers, staff members from the hospital obstetrical unit. They'd heard about the fetus with no brain.

The baby's shoulder got wedged in as she was trapped behind my pelvic bone, the obstetrician explained. He told me that the fetus wasn't coming out, but it had descended too far down into the birth canal for him to be able to perform a C-section. He also informed me that at that point there was nothing he could do to dislodge the fetus. He quite seriously directed me: "You have to find a way to get her out."

All I knew to do was to pray. Ten minutes later she was delivered. They took her away immediately, and then returned her dressed in an infant's gown and a cap on her head to conceal the missing skull. I took her in my arms and as I held her, I could feel the presence of one who is alive. This was my daughter, a living and breathing person, despite her lack of a brain. I placed my forefinger into her tiny hand and in response, her fingers clasped around mine.

"That's just an automatic, neurological response," I was told by one of the physicians. "Not an indication of an actual living person." Perhaps that was true, in physiological terms. But as a spiritual matter, what I felt that afternoon was the presence of a beautiful, living being.

When the earlier message had come through me regarding the time our baby was to be born, neither the nurses nor my husband knew what to make of it. In fact, our daughter was born at 5:20, over two hours after the stated time of 3:12 p.m. They probably assumed that my incorrect proclamation was due to a delusional state of mind, a result of hard laboring, or the duress of anticipating my child's fate.

Happily for me, and as required by the organ donation protocol, our baby was born alive. It was important and meaningful to me to be able to hold her, albeit only for very briefly. Because of arrangements we had made for her organs to be donated at the time of death, and the complex protocol involved, she was taken from my arms very quickly, whisked from the delivery room, and transported by ambulance to the neonatal intensive care unit of the university hospital across town. I sobbed when I heard the ambulance driving away, my shoulders heaving,

41

its siren blaring. Within less than a half an hour, our daughter would be intubated, and placed in an incubator.

On the third day after our daughter's birth, we received a call from the intensive care unit at the university hospital. They were asking us to come in. When my husband and I arrived, the unit head of Pediatrics explained that the staff no longer felt comfortable giving our baby the treatments needed to keep her alive. When we were led behind a curtain where the incubator held our newborn, my husband took one look at all the wires and tubes attached to and inside her body and said, "I don't know if she is struggling to live or to die."

It was time to let her go. We were asked to step back into the waiting area while the procedure was done to disconnect the life support. When we were called back inside, and she was pronounced dead, my husband pointed up at the clock on the wall, which read 3:12 pm. The time I'd announced as for birth was actually the time of her death. Which meant, to me, that there was no "death."

We'd selected "Zoe" as our baby's name early in the first trimester, assuming that our child would be a daughter. My husband and I first discovered it as a character's name, in a Woody Allen film called *New York Stories*, and we liked the sound of it. Looking up its meaning in a baby name book, we learned that Zoe is the Greek word meaning *life*. That suited us just fine. I have since discovered that for Christianity, the name has biblical significance, when Jesus referred to himself by saying, "Eaimi he zoe," meaning, "I am life." Might Zoe's soul have been that of my Mom Mom, the grandmother who asked permission to "come back" through me? I suppose that is possible but I had no clear sense of Zoe as being her. Furthermore, it's probably best that I didn't know.

I recently learned something important about that, when communicating with Gitana, a horse in the Costa Rican herd that I often visit. Gitana gave birth to a foal called Arenal (named after the nearby volcano). Arenal was born just under a year after another horse in the herd had died. That horse's name was Stella. Her life ended tragically when she got her head stuck in the rails of a farm fence. Her desperate struggle to get free from the fence caused irreparable damage to her head and neck, and her life could not be saved. Judging by their behavior as described to me, the herd was deeply disturbed by her loss, especially those who witnessed it. As was Debbie, the caretaker-owner of the herd, shocked and grieved by Stella's death. In communicating with him, a horse named Cosmo suggested that Arenal is, in fact, Stella reborn. He said that the herd was trying to help Arenal to adjust to his new life. Debbie asked me to check directly with Arenal on that.

As I approached the young horse I expressed the intention of serving the highest good, as I offer whenever I communicate as an equine empath. The first answer I received was not from the foal but, rather, from an enlightened source that comes through "the still small voice" inside of me. It instructed, "Ask Debbie why she needs this information."

Debbie thought for a moment and then replied,

"I am curious because this horse already knows everything, such as the different gestures used in the Parelli games. We haven't even taught him those, and yet he responds correctly when we use them. But I really don't need to know whether or not this is Stella."

Guided by that same voice I continued as led, explaining that it's important for Arenal to be allowed to develop in the fullness of his being, without preconceptions of his identity.

That Stella's life is over and even if this young horse has imbibed her soul, it no longer expresses as Stella, and it is here to experience life as an altogether different being. The voice stressed the importance of Debbie seeing Arenal as he is now in order for him to thrive. Gitana, the foal's mother told us that Arenal is having difficulty adjusting to his life. And that he has been confused as to his identity. Debbie nodded knowingly as she heard that, explaining that for his first two months of his life Arenal had been unusually sickly, and had to be put on an IV drip. Gitana said also that she has not bonded well with the foal, partly because Stella never left the herd after her death. And that mothering Arenal is like being mother to a sister. Stella's soul suddenly lunged from spirit into body right after Arenal was born, she explained.

Debbie shared that this was apparent in Gitana's nonchalant behavior towards him, and that in the beginning Arenal nursed at the tits of Suzie, the horse that had been mother to Stella. Which means Cosmo had been correct; the herd was trying to help Arenal settle into his life as this new being. Clearly it was important that Debbie, the stablemen and trainers release Stella and see Arenal as Arenal. As I will explain further in Part II, this same lesson came to me more directly, and personally, in a healing session I had in Italy.

My daughter Kaya was born with a scar across her lower abdomen. I hadn't noticed it until a visit to the pediatrician's office at the age of one month, when the nurse specifically asked when and why colon surgery had been performed on her. "What surgery?" I returned. The nurse pointed to the scar from her navel to waist as indicative of such. About five years later, I found some photos of ancestors, put them in frames and displayed them on a shelf in our living room. When my husband saw the photo of my great aunt Norma, as a child of about the same age as Kaya, he gasped and said, "That's my little girl!" The resemblance was shocking to us all. Interestingly, Norma died from colon cancer. Surgery was attempted but when they opened her to find the extent of the metastasized growth, they stitched her back up and sent her home where she died shortly thereafter.

The research is extensive and there are plenty of books documenting cases of reincarnation, so I need not attempt to do so here. My point in sharing these stories is that during the pregnancy with Zoe it did cross my mind that my grandmother may have wanted to return as that child. Whether or not that was the case, it may be best for all concerned if that information remains obscure. What is important is Zoe's life and how profoundly it affected me. The pregnancy, Zoe's birth, and especially her death, served to open my heart to a depth of empathy that has been with me ever since. Was that change in me, from emotionally numb to deeply empathetic, due to a grandmother's love; a choice of her soul to help me to grow as a human being? Perhaps so, but for whatever it was, and whoever *she* was, I am truly grateful. But losing her was devastating.

Despite the inevitability of Zoe's death, it was a shock to leave the hospital for home without her, and I was unable to grieve for a very long time. I continued my meditation and chanting practices daily over the following weeks, but it didn't help much. My heart was broken, I was depressed, and I no longer felt satisfied in my spiritual life. Then one morning, as awakening from a night's sleep, I saw a vivid image of a very young male child, with glistening eyes and a beaming smile. He was beautiful to me and seeing him brought an immense sense of joy. "Don't be sad," he said. "I'm coming, soon."

Not long after that I was up again and back to work. But first I disassembled the nursery we had prepared for our newborn baby. We'd waited until the pregnancy was well into the last trimester, just in case, and then purchased the crib, bedding, and various other newborn baby devices. The room was decorated beautifully with cheerful wallpaper on the walls; an antique-style maple wood crib, with lofty yellow bed coverings; fanciful wall hangings of animals and matching rugs; and a handmade, colorful, cloth hot air balloon hanging from the window. I boxed it all and put it away for a future child. Then I flew to upstate New York and spent a weekend at the Siddha Yoga Ashram.

There were probably 800 people gathered there to be with Swami Chidvilasananda (Gurumayi), successor to Muktananda after he had passed. One evening most of us were sitting silently in the darkened meditation hall. From out of the silence I heard an eerily haunting sound. Someone was wailing, loudly, and mournfully so. I listened to her for a moment before I realized that the woman wailing was none other than me. The grieving process had finally begun. My newborn child had died.

Rumi's poem, *The Desire and Importance of Failing*, includes the verses:

> *You know how it is. Sometimes*
> *we plan a trip to one place,*
> *but something takes us to another.*
> *When a horse is being broken, the trainer*
> *pulls it in many different directions,*
> *so the horse will come to know*
> *what it is to be ridden.*

The most beautiful and alert horse is one
completely attuned to the rider.
God fixes a passionate desire in you,
and then disappoints you.
God does that a hundred times!

For a while I was adrift in my spiritual path and religious practice, although I continued daily meditation practices, and sometimes still chanted the Gurugita. Then one morning I woke with clear memory of a dream: I was the sole passenger in a car driven by Gurumayi (Swami Chidvilasananda). We seemed to be heading for a magnificent palace-like structure that I could see in the distance. But before we got there Gurumayi pulled the car over to the side of the road and stopped. "Get out," she demanded of me. I was surprised and shocked, but did as I was told. She then drove away. My interpretation of that dream was that I would have to take responsibility for myself in my spiritual journey. She was letting me know that she was no longer going to be "in the driver's seat." Or perhaps my subconscious was letting me know that I no longer needed that kind of religious structure.

I boxed up my guru photos, Hindu god figurines, malas (mantra repetition beads), and other worship paraphernalia, and put those away in a closet. Work became my primary focus. I also returned to the university to pursue a PhD in religious studies with a focus on bio-ethics. In part because of complex bioethical issues involved, our efforts to donate Zoe's organs were unsuccessful. What I believed to be the right thing to do turned out to be wrong, ethically speaking. I'd hoped that through formal study I would come to understand why.

One night, after a long day of work and classes, as I fell asleep I heard an orchestra playing. Only it wasn't like any orchestra I'd ever heard, with recognizable strings, brass, woodwinds, and a percussion section. The composition was mesmerizing, and the instrumentation was surreal, hauntingly beautiful, exciting yet sublime. As I listened further, and began to fall deeper into sleep, I felt more alert than any waking state I've known. What I was hearing was not coming as input to my eardrums, it was coming from inside the vast, deep, darkness inside of me, music I could hear and also feel, that gave me a sense of coming from very far away, and intimately close at the same time. When I woke the next morning I could not recall the sound, only that I had heard it. I never heard it again, though it remained with me as a source of encouragement, that there was infinitely more to the universe than I had realized.

No longer devoted to a guru, or following the Siddha Yoga teachings, I returned to the local Friends Meeting I had discovered in college. Supported by their worship community, I would continue my quest for union with God, not through a guru, but directly, turning inward the focus of my desire to unify with God.

About a year later I made the decision to try another pregnancy. This time, however, I conceded to having a sonogram, which revealed that it was a boy. I also agreed to have the "alpha-fetal protein" blood test done, which would reveal possibilities of a neural tube defect in the fetus. But I still struggled with the notion of prenatal testing, because I didn't know what I would do with the information if it turned out that this child was also afflicted. And I knew I'd be counseled to abort if the blood work suggested a neural tube defect.

Two months into the pregnancy I was advised to have amniocentesis, a procedure that involves inserting a needle into the uterus and withdrawing amniotic fluid for testing. I was informed that the chances of losing the child due to the procedure itself were about the same chance as the child having a neural tube defect. This put me into a quandary, though ultimately I was convinced that having the test was the wisest decision. On the day of the procedure I came home from the hospital and lay quietly on the couch, moving as little as possible so as not to disturb the fetus, whose protected home inside my body had just been invaded. When no spontaneous abortion followed in the next few weeks, I breathed more deeply, with relief. It all turned out all right, and the baby boy fetus thrived and grew into a full-term pregnancy. But my fear of losing another baby had gripped me, unknowingly.

At forty weeks gestation my cervix dilated, signally the impending birth, but the contractions never progressed. I labored for nearly ten hours until finally the obstetrical nurse "broke my water" with a plastic rod. A few hours later when there was still no birth, my husband realized what was happening.

"You've got to let this baby be born," he said. "Stop trying to protect him."

My response was tears. To my irrational mind and mothering heart, I figured that as long as the baby was inside of my womb, he'd be safe. I knew from past experience that his birth could mean something horrid. Finally I let go, and before long a beautiful wide-eyed baby, with a full head of black hair, was suckling at my breast; such a feeling of sublime joy it was for me.

When I went into labor with my daughter, three years later, I knew what I should not do. I trusted that she would be born okay, and tried to relax in the process. But when the contractions became particularly painful I told Claudia, the nurse midwife, that I wanted to leave the hospital and go back home. And I meant it; the pain was too much for me to handle. Claudia looked me in the eyes and said,

"Your body has millions of years of information in its cells, telling it exactly what to do. So let go and let your body birth this baby."

It was the first time I remember being taught that I could and should trust my body. I'd always seen my body as separate from "me," but had not considered that it, rather than "I," was in control. I wanted to trust the midwife's wisdom, but I was afraid, and tense. Seeing that, Claudia asked if I'd like to chant the mantra with her. She, too, had experienced Swami Muktananda in her twenties, and remembered that as being something we shared. Together we sang "Om namah Shivaya," repeating the words softly, sweetly, melodically, until I completely relaxed.

An hour later (by then my husband had arrived), my daughter began her final descent through the birth canal. An altered state of consciousness took hold of me and I began to sing. Only this time, the words were neither Sanskrit nor English, but a language totally unfamiliar to me, and to my husband. And the melody was one I'd never heard before. My singing voice carried loud enough to bring two nurses in the hallway to the delivery room the door. Peeking inside they explained that they'd heard the unusual sounds, and were curious to know what was going on. My husband answered that he had no idea. And neither did I. But it felt to me as if the singing was announcing my daughter's imminent arrival, her soul accompanied by the unseen beings that were singing around me, with, or maybe through me. What it actually was remains a mystery.

III

Breathe Through Your Feet

FROM DEEP SLEEP I sat up with a start, wide-awake and announcing, "It's time for me to run a school!" My husband, sleeping by my side, stirred a bit and said, "Okay," before falling back to sleep. The prompting was direct and clear, although I cannot say what was the source of the leading other than "that which guides me."

Shortly thereafter, I learned that a local independent school was searching for a new head. I applied, was interviewed, and made the final cut, but decided to withdraw from the search. "What am I doing?" I chided myself. My husband and I agreed that I already had too much on my plate. Running a school would take too much time and energy, and it would be enormously stressful given that I had an infant and toddler to care for, and was enrolled in a PhD program.

Within a few weeks of pulling out of the search, I contracted a kidney stone. Fortunately it passed quickly, but shortly thereafter I developed acid reflux. My doctor was able to treat that readily, only to have me return a week later complaining of heart palpitations.

"What is going on with you?" she asked. "I mean, really going on?"

"I withdrew from a search for a position that I might have been destined for," I explained with an upwelling of emotion.

On that same day I was scheduled to meet over lunch with the school's chair of the board of trustees. During our meal she invited me to join the board. I asked her what had happened with the head of school search, and whom they'd hired for the position. She conveyed that I had been their top candidate, and when I pulled out, the board decided to reopen the search. They'd be appointing an interim for the job that very night. I knew what I had to do. "Never mind about me coming on the board" I exclaimed. "If the board is still interested, then I'll reconsider stepping into the head of school position."

The process was quick. I signed the contract and gave notice of resignation from my university administration position. Two weeks later the outgoing chair of the board of trustees asked me to attend an executive board meeting in his home. Propped up on the easel in his den was a graph that compared admissions trends of the local schools. As I listened to him speak, I began to realize the implications of what was written on that whiteboard. And I tried to come to terms with the decision I'd made to leave my secure job. It was too late to turn back at that point.

"This is a failing institution," he declared, pointing to the lines indicating how the other local schools were rising in enrollment, while ours was falling precipitously. He also spoke of lacking resources. I had not realized that the school was in such dire financial position, possibly on the brink of closure. When I interviewed for the job, I hadn't known enough to ask for recent financial statements or annual reports. I'd simply followed what I thought was "a leading," which in Quaker parlance means to be moved by God to act in some way. I'd made the decision to NOT take the job, in a process of careful discernment. I changed my mind and accepted it when my body began to break down, indicating that it was a mistake to have turned away from the leading.

I lay awake that night, wondering whether I'd made a terrible decision. As my children slept soundly in their rooms, and my husband beside me in our bed, I rose and went to our bedroom window. Looking out over the moonlit pond in our backyard I whispered a prayer,

"Holy Spirit: I'm afraid. I don't know what to do about this school, and I'm afraid that I may fail them."

"You will fail if you try to do this by yourself," the still small voice replied, "You are not alone. Everything that you need will come to you just when it is needed."

And indeed it did.

Within the first few weeks of my arrival, the board challenged me to articulate a vision for the future of the school, one that could help revitalize the institution. But before I could get to that, my first task was to deal with the break-in that had happened on the second day in the job. Someone had smashed the windows of my office on the night before, entered the building and vandalized my desk in the process. It was a mess and I immediately informed the police, and also the press. The culprit, it turns out, was a boy named Joe. He'd seen me on the local news that night, threatening to penalize whoever had done it. Then he showed up the next morning to confess and ask for my forgiveness. Joe explained to me that he was angry about being suspended by the previous head of school. He had no idea that a new head had been hired. We worked it out and Joe made amends through manual labor around the school's grounds. Believing him to be a good, well-intentioned young man, I decided to invite Joe back to the school. He enrolled again that September and was doing well. Then later that autumn Joe ended his life by hanging. My responsibility as head was to help the school through this shocking loss.

At his funeral the casket was left open. I waited in the long line to view the body. As I arrived at the casket I whispered, "Go in peace, Joe."

"Help me," I heard a voice say in return. I knew intuitively that those words had to be coming from Joe. His stiff body was cradled in the red satin lining, a checkered kerchief around his neck to conceal the violent wound that caused his death. Joe was nearby, but he was not in that coffin, nor was he alive in the sense that we commonly understand.

"Help you, how?" I returned, using the silent voice of my subtler faculties.

"I didn't know it would be so permanent!" Joe exclaimed. "Please help me to get back inside my body."

It was very sad. What could I possibly do? In an altered state, driven perhaps by an irrational, emotional rage, the young man had tied a noose around his neck and kicked away the chair that held him up, not realizing what it would actually mean to die.

"This is final," I tell him in the silence of our exchange. "That body in the coffin is no longer available to you."

I moved away, so that others in line could have their turn at viewing the body. But I just couldn't leave Joe in such purgatory. He'd reached out to me, one soul to another, through the senses beyond those considered normal. I took a seat in the corner of the room, where I wouldn't be obvious to other mourners. I sensed that Joe had followed me there, and was standing at my side. I closed my eyes, envisioning a tunnel of light, and pointed in its direction.

"Over there, Joe. Can you see the light?" I whispered while holding onto the vision. "Go that way. It's your way back home." And with that, Joe was gone.

Joe was the first of two suicides that occurred in the course of my five-year tenure at the school, both hangings by teenage boys. For the handful of girls who were apparently struggling, their issues were related to depression, eating disorders, and self-mutilation by cutting. Most of the school's students were healthy and thriving, but the institution itself was not. It took a great deal of stamina, focus, energy, and time for me to keep up with the demands of the job.

My main priority, as stipulated by the board of trustees, was to raise money for the school. But I'd never done that before and wasn't particularly comfortable with the notion of asking people to donate money. The school had a development director but she'd moved on. I was told by the board to launch a capital campaign, but I had no clue where to begin. One afternoon while in my office, my administrative assistant called to say a visitor wanted to see me. She did not have an appointment but had simply seen the sign for the school as she drove by, and decided to stop in. I was not inclined to interrupt my day with such a random intrusion. But on my assistant's prompting, I said okay.

The woman was driving through on her way further south to Georgia. She was a development professional and being between jobs, had some free time on her hands.

We sat together on the couch in my office as she explained about her background and experience with raising money. And then she said, "Is there any way I can be of help to you, as a volunteer? I have a few weeks to spare."

I told her what the board had asked of me, of my total lack of experience, and my discomfort with the idea of asking people for money. Her reply was something like this:

"First you should understand that people with the means to give, are wanting to give, and waiting to be inspired by a cause they can believe in. Your job is to offer them that opportunity. I will teach you how to do that. I will also conduct a feasibility study for you, so you know who to ask and for how much."

Five weeks later, the capital campaign was launched. As for the mysterious woman who showed up that day and helped me, she left town and I never heard from her again.

The fundraising process meant that I became publically engaged and personally very exposed, in the school and also the larger community. Many people knew who I was and, most anytime I ventured into public places around town, I'd run into someone associated with the school, or someone who was simply curious about the work I was doing there. Because our family home was located in the heart of the downtown area, it was especially difficult to maintain a sense of personal privacy.

We were wonderfully successful in raising money and building new buildings with it. But over time the position began to take its toll on me, physically and emotionally. For well over a year I searched for just the right place to retreat. On weekends, whenever possible, I'd persuade my husband to come with me, to look at various rural properties on the market. One evening at a school fundraising function for my school, I mentioned to a former head my desire to find a getaway property. He acknowledged my desire and said he understood. Another year went by, with employment and family responsibilities mounting, until finally

I burned out. Emotionally drained and energetically depleted, I sought help from a shamanic healer friend named Laura. I shared with her my vision of a refuge from the intense, public life that was my world, a private place somewhere in a natural setting where I could tune out, relax, and rejuvenate myself.

"Why don't you ask the trees to help you find a place?" Laura asked.

Her suggestion was baffling; I asked her to explain.

"Find a tree that attracts you, and place an offering around its base such as tobacco or corn meal. Then ask the tree to help you find the land that you are seeking. The tree will send a message to other trees that will help you in your search."

Laura was known as someone who had studied with Native American elders, and had walked as an "Earth steward" for many years, listening to and developing communicative capacities with the natural world. To me, Laura's counsel felt right. Anyway, what did I have to lose by trying? I purchased a package of tobacco and set out in search of just the right tree. Not knowing exactly what kind to look for, or where I might find it, I figured I'd know when I saw it. I drove about fifteen miles from my home before spotting it: a mighty oak, probably 150 feet high, and perhaps as many years old. It was located on private property not too far from the primary dwelling, which was a majestic antebellum brick home with a two-storied front porch and a circular driveway. I couldn't tell if anyone was living there, so I took a risk and pulled off the road, crossing the front lawn on foot to get to the tree. I stood in acknowledgement of the tree's beauty and strength. Noticing what I felt inside of me while in its presence, I knew this was the right tree for my purposes. Perhaps it was my imagination, but I got the feeling the tree was also sensing me.

Encircling its trunk while sprinkling tobacco along the base, I spoke:

Hello, mighty Oak. I've come to ask for your help. I am looking for a piece of land where I can go and be whenever I need to restore myself, a place that will be a refuge from my public life, where Nature is at center and provides a source of support and replenishment for me and all those who spend time there. I'm told that you can spread the word to other trees that I am looking for this land. I'd be grateful for any help you and other trees would be willing to give.

Leaning my back against the tree I closed my eyes, trying to imagine what such a piece of land would feel like, and envisioning a sweet little cottage on it where I could go to rest, and spend quiet time.

That was it. I drove away.

Three days later I received a phone call. It was from Bill, the former head I'd met at the fundraising event the year before. Our conversation went something like this:

"Hi, it's Bill Porter calling."

"Oh, hi Bill."

"Did you ever find that piece of land you were looking for?"

"No, not yet."

"Well, I was driving home and noticed a "for sale by owner" sign being put up today. It's for a piece of land out on Milton Road. I remembered our conversation and am calling to let you know, assuming that you're still looking."

I knew that property wouldn't last too long, so I drove out right away to get the details from the sign, told my husband about it, and then called for an appointment to see it. The next afternoon we walked that property with its owner. Normally I'd be anxious in waist-tall, tick-infested grass. But the land felt so good that I harbored no such fears. The land was a knoll overlooking a distant river, with 360-degree views of the surrounding farms and hills. To say the least, the vistas were arresting. We put in a full-price offer that evening and it was accepted. Good timing: three other offers came in the next day. We built a small retreat cottage on the land for weekend use. Eventually we built a larger home and moved there to live on the land full time. Perhaps it was all a coincidence, but I don't believe that: so thank you, trees!

Our school community hosted a tribeswoman from the Metepenagiag Mi'kmaq Nation of New Brunswick, Canada, as an assembly speaker. She told of how plants sense and feel human beings, and how they actually respond to humans. She challenged the students to perform their own experiment: To acquire and treat two plants of the same species exactly the same. They were to water and feed them the same amount, at the same time each week, and keep them next to each other on the same surface, so that they would be exposed to identical light, moisture, and other environmental factors. The only difference was to be that one plant would be treated with affection, offered praising verbal attention, while the other was to be completely ignored, except for providing its basic care.

She said, "Tell that plant how beautiful you think it is, how happy you are to have it in your home, and how much it delights you. Then wait and see what happens."

She told the students to note any differences between the growth and productivity of the two plants. This would be a good experiment and the students would learn something about the sensitivities of plants. I smiled as she spoke, having already learned a lesson from the trees about their intelligence and sensitivity. What I had not yet learned was that my own body is also a living, intelligent organism, sensitive to its surroundings, able to communicate with other living bodies, and especially with me. If only I'd sorted that out earlier, and been able to heed its warnings and messages, my marriage might have had a better chance.

There were so many signs: the sensation of my throat closing when I was holding back what needed to be spoken; the lack of response when being touched; the asthmatic breathing when I felt powerless; the sensation of being disembodied. Even in childhood, I was inept at using body awareness in feeling my way through. When it might have hurt too much or been too frightening, my choice was always to leave it, rising up into (and often out of) my skull where I could always think, and analyze my situation, without having to actually feel what my body was telling me.

It wasn't until my fourth year as head of school that I came to realize how little bodily awareness I had, or that my body could be an instrument of self-awareness and understanding. I knew lots about how to eat well, and was very attentive to what I fed my family. The importance of exercise was also clear. I hadn't smoked a cigarette in decades and avoided excessive use of alcohol. But since young adulthood, my priority and focus of attention day to day had been on the demands of my schooling or my work, and on my spiritual practices, leaving little room for attentiveness to my body-self as a living, sensing entity. In fact, I was going numb.

On particularly intense days at the school, for example, I would ignore the impulse to relieve my bladder, feeling myself to be under more important pressures like taking the telephone calls of an irate parent, anxious board member, or potential major donor. I usually worked through lunch at my desk, never could afford the "luxury" of exercise because I didn't have the time, and often forgot to take a breath. As for the awareness of my body in intimate encounters with my husband, I could barely feel anything. Sometimes, in the throes of a panic attack, I couldn't feel my body at all and I'd surmise that maybe I had died, or was unconscious somewhere lying in a coma and dreaming the life I was leading; the thought of which would cause my heart to pound in my chest, and only then did I know I was still alive.

I'd hired an assistant named Claire, who was evidently more aware of my disembodied state than I. Claire would sometimes put her hands on my shoulders and say to me, "Breathe through your feet, and feel the ground, knowing that the earth is supporting you."

In the midst of this pressured life, a friend named Karen contracted brain cancer. She put up a long and vigorous fight, ending with her in a coma, being cared for round the clock in her home. I went to see her, the likelihood of her approaching death on my mind. I didn't understand that her family had hired nursing but not hospice care, believing she would still recover. On my arrival I was shown to Karen's bedside. Her eyes were closed and she did not indicate any capacity to respond as I stood by her, recounting out loud memories of times we had spent together. When I spoke words about the end of life, I was quickly ushered away, scolded for speaking of this. I was surprised and a bit shocked, but respected the family wishes when told to leave the home. I got into my car to drive away, sensing that Karen had come with me. Her presence in spirit was palpable as if she were there beside me.

I was still feeling Karen when I pulled into the driveway of my own home. So I closed my eyes, whispered that I knew she was there, and listened. She'd wanted to acknowledge my visit, and to let me know that despite her family's denial she was well aware of her dying state. She also wanted to share the memories I spoke of, and to say goodbye to me.

About a week later Karen passed away.

As I continued to work hard as head of school, I was also caring for my family, writing a dissertation to complete the graduate program in bioethics I'd enrolled in when Zoe died, and active in the Quaker Meeting; all of which took priority over my physical self, of which I was hardly aware. But I must have been under the care and support of "guardians" who were helping me: this became apparent on the day of my annual appointment with an endocrinologist. I was having a frenetic day, and running late. My appointment was at 4:30, the last one scheduled for the pituitary clinic that closed at 5:00. I hopped into my car at 4:25, speeding along the interstate, well aware of how late I would be. I parked my car and ran through the hospital corridors, arriving at the clinic at 4:45. (This was before cell phones.) The nurse who I'd known for many years greeted me.

"I am so sorry. Is it too late to be seen?" I asked her, panting.

"Calm down now. Don't worry. Dr. Thorner is waiting for you. He knows you are running late."

"But how does he know that?" I asked, perplexed.

"Because of the man who came by here a couple of minutes ago, and told us you were on your way."

"What man?" I asked. No one knew about my appointment, not my assistant, neither my father nor mother, not even my husband. I could not fathom to whom she was referring. "I don't understand," I exclaimed. "No one knew I was coming here.

"Really?" she replied. "Well someone must have known."

"A man was just here, you say?

"That's right," she affirmed.

"What did he look like?" I asked.

After she described an elderly, brown-skinned man, I headed around the corner in search of who it may have been. The nurse, realizing what must have happened smiled and said, "I wouldn't bother looking for *him*."

Overall, I was a healthy person who very rarely got sick, and from that I tended to assume that all was well. It was the erratic, breathless flutters of my heart (diagnosed as atrial fibrillation after wearing a monitor on my chest) that first got my attention. But apparently that wasn't enough to bring me into full awareness, to consciously inhabit my body-self. So I pushed on, status quo, in keen awareness of the world around me, responding to its demands, and any "leadings" I discerned to be of Spirit. I worked intense, long days, consumed by external pressures and centered in my thinking mind, except when in meditative silence or prayer, during which time my attention was on feeling and hearing God. It was the aching, burning sensations across my back and shoulders, down my arms, and in my neck from an inflammatory response, along with the intermittent chronic fatigue, and erratic sleep, which finally became the audible voice of an orphaned body, desperately trying to get my attention. It took the onset of fibromyalgia to finally get me to pay attention. The time had come when I had no choice but to devote time to self-care.

Exhausted, I resigned from the head of school position and took an entire summer to heal. With a change in diet to omit nightshade foods, weekly acupuncture sessions, vitamin and plant nutrition supplements such as Noni juice, daily lap swimming, a weekly Chi Gong class, and allowing myself to sleep for as long as needed each day, I did recover from the fibromyalgia. But how quickly one forgets.

IV

It's Spring and Finally I Have No Will

IT WAS THE MONTH of March. I'd worked for seven years as an assistant professor and was promoted to associate. Now I was on sabbatical leave, taking time away from home, on a writing retreat at Hedgebrook in Washington State. Cloudy days prevailed there on Whidbey Island.

One grey day while sitting at the desk, working on my novel and pondering the construction of a sentence, the sun shined brightly into the bay window. That's how it could be there; for days in a row the sky would be gray, and then suddenly, rays of sunlight would stream through a slit in the cloud cover. I saved the document I was working on, slid back in the chair and stood up. This was the opportunity I'd been waiting for. I removed my clothing, put on a bathrobe, and slipped into a pair of shoes. Laying a blanket over my arm, I grabbed a water bottle, a pen, and a notebook, and then walked out the door of the cabin named Owl.

The woods were quiet that afternoon, as usual. No one else seemed to be outside. Most likely, the other six women in residence were still inside their cabins writing. I walked the path among the wildlife, bushes, and trees, becoming increasingly aware of being alone out there, which evoked a sense of vulnerability in me. Indeed, the land was isolated; but since it was the private property of Hedgebrook, a retreat for women writers, I trusted that I'd be safe. Except of course for the lions, and tigers, and bears – oh, my!

Before long I reached a glade where the tree canopy gave way to a wide-open sky above a small grassy meadow. The space felt just right for my purposes; I wanted to sunbathe in the nude. I spread out my blanket, removed my robe, and lay myself down. The ground was hard and bumpy under my back, and the cool air brought a tingle to my bare skin. But as the sun's rays intensified, my chill diminished. I felt great out there, relaxed and free, while three thousand miles away my children and husband carried on with the activities and demands of life back home. How fortunate for me that I'd been granted the time and opportunity to do nothing but write, in a quiet, natural setting. In gratitude, I closed my eyes and allowed my mind to wander. Just as I was beginning to doze off, my attention was drawn to the trill of a bird. I glanced over at the trees to where the sound seemed to be coming from. That's when I distinctively heard a voice say, "There's a gift here for you."

"How odd," I thought, lifting myself onto my elbows and searching to find the source of the voice. But I could see no one anywhere nearby.

"There's a gift here for you," I heard again, as if spoken by an invisible person right there with me. It didn't frighten me; I was more intrigued.

"Really?" I replied almost childlike, eager to discover something special, something just for me. I rolled onto my side. "Where?" I asked out loud, running my hand over the grasses within reaching distance. Suddenly I felt a stinging sensation along my forearm. It hurt and I panicked, not knowing the cause of the pain.

"Maybe it was a snake and I've been bitten," was my first thought. I threw on my robe, grabbed my belongings, and took off running barefoot through the woods. When I spotted the cabin of a fellow writer, a physician, I headed for her door and banged hard.

"I think something has stung or bitten me but I don't know what," I said panting, the moment she greeted me. The panic in my eyes must have been obvious. Gently taking my arm into her hands, she rubbed her fingers across the inflamed skin and smiled knowingly.

"I think you're going to live," she reassured me with a smirk. I listened intently to her further explanation.

"What a relief," I sighed, admitting it was my imagination, rather than venom, that had gotten to me. I'd never heard of the stinging nettle plant. Apparently it was the time of the year when nettles emerge. I happened to be lying right beside a young patch of it. *There's a gift here for you,* the voice had said. Was *that* supposed to be the gift?

At our Hedgebrook community dinner that evening, I shared my saga with our cook. She pulled a book down from the shelf above where her pots and pans were hung. Handing it to me she offered, "Let's look it up in here."

We found in it a section that relayed the nutritional qualities of the offending plant.

Urtica Dioica, also known as stinging nettle: Nettles contain high levels of protein, calcium, phosphorus, iron, magnesium, and beta-carotene and high amounts of the vitamins A, C, D, and B complex and can be used to treat a variety of ailments including allergies and stiff joints.

I read on about its nutritionally nourishing, though cutaneous pain-inducing leaves and stems, realizing what a boon it was to discover the plant in its wild state. Every day for the remainder of my retreat I foraged for young nettles, making tea from what I harvested and drinking it morning and night to quiet my sniffles and sneezes. I also made poultices, placing them on my back, in finding that the nettles brought relief from the persistent aches of sciatica I'd been suffering with. The unexpected benefit was an increase of energy; it seems to have also addressed my anemia.

It remains a mystery to me what or who spoke those words, "There is a gift here for you," and how I was able to hear them. Could it have been the plants that were communicating with me? Some scientists see plants as information processing organisms, with the capacity for complex communication between individual plants. In retrospect, having looked into plant neurobiology research, I wonder whether the forest itself functions as an organism, with the capacity for complex communication with other beings, including me? As far-fetched and fantastical as the idea that plants communicate with humans may seem, is there a better explanation for what happened on Whidbey Island?

After returning from Hedgebrook I continued my writing retreat at home. For the next three months I followed nearly the same routine as I did on Whidbey Island:

Awake before dawn; slip quietly out of the house and cross the grassy path to the cottage; make a fire in the wood stove; sit for meditation and prayers; write, write, write, taking breaks for a

simple midday meal and cup of tea; return to the house early in
the evening to prepare dinner for the family; eat with my husband
and children; go back to the cottage for evening writing; meditate;
go to bed and sleep

Except during family meals, I spent the retreat time mostly in silence. I rarely left our property, or encountered another person, other than my immediate family members. In aiming to be supportive, my husband did most of the grocery shopping and chauffeured our children to their activities. For me it was truly a retreat from the active world "out there," with few worries or anxieties. The spaces around me, inside and out, began to provide a sense of comforting seclusion. Each morning I stepped out of our home, barefoot, and wrapped in a shawl, the sounds of chirping crickets, and the dew sparkling under the first rays of the sun as I scurried across the grass to the cottage. I continued my retreat with a sense of tranquility.

Tucked into the corner of the cottage was my personal altar, a simple surface with a beeswax candle and incense burner, and a few items of meaning to me: a cross, a quartz crystal, and a piece of lava that Pele gave me permission to take from Kilauea in Hawaii. With candle lit and incense burning, when I knelt before it I truly meant the words I uttered, "Thank you, Holy Spirit, for this new day."

It felt as if I'd relinquished the need and sense of control over my life and world, and existed in a state of complete grace. My inner world took on a joyful awareness, and peace. I knew of what the ecstatic poets had written. I understood what Martin Luther King meant when he said, "Occasionally in life there are those moments of unutterable fulfillment which cannot be completely explained by those symbols called words. Their meanings can only be articulated by the inaudible language of the heart."

I seemed to be living what Jesus meant by, "My peace I give to you; not as the world gives do I give to you." Until, that is, life took a sudden and tumultuous turn, and robbed me of my sublime state of mind.

It was a week before our son's high school spring break, two months before his graduation from high school. He'd come home one night, after socializing with friends, announcing that he had not slept at all that weekend. I didn't know what to make of this disclosure, but it caused me to worry. I slept restlessly that night. The next morning Ari left for school, having again remained awake most the night. In the afternoon I received a text from his cell phone, so I assumed that it was a message from him. Except that the sentences were confusing, and seemed to say that he was leaving for New York City, plans I knew nothing about and that didn't make sense. Who was he going with? Where was he going to stay? Why was he going there? I replied to his message by asking those questions. What returned was a rapid series of five or six additional messages, all written in gibberish.

I was working at home that day, preparing a lecture for class. My husband was also working at home. I was alarmed by the texts, as was he, so we decided to go immediately to our son's school. When we arrived my husband went straight to the principal's office and I stepped out into the hall. The bell had just rung and classes were changing. Scores of students were moving in both directions along the corridor. I turned to my left, and there he was coming down the hall heading in my direction. I watched as he approached, noting the oddly jovial look on his face, his spry gait, and that wild expression in his eyes as he spoke out loud, perhaps to someone nearby. When Ari saw me he waved, and as he approached asked, "What are you doing here?" I did not recognize him as the son we'd known for seventeen years.

The wait was long at the hospital emergency room that afternoon. He could hardly sit still; he had to get going to New York City. It was evening before they'd secured a bed for him in 5-East, the psychiatric unit of the university hospital. The diagnosis given was bi-polar disorder, and he'd be started on lithium, sleeping pills, a calmative, and an antipsychotic right away. My blood pressure had always been low, around 118 over 80. That night it shot up to 140/110: frightening over terrified. The body always tells the truth; mine told of panic, my nervous system hyper-engaged in an acute state of fight or flight. But whom could I battle, and where could I run, to protect my child and our family from the looming threat of this chronic condition?

His hospitalization would have been for at least ten days. But I could not tolerate his being there alone with strangers, sleeping in a stark white room under a camera's watch, pacing the hallway that led from one patient room to the next, back and forth like a caged animal. My son was behind locked doors, with no access to the fresh air, sunlight, rolling green hills and country roads that would help him to remember who he was. I pleaded with the resident psychiatrist to release him, insisting that he would be better off at home. She asked me if someone would be there around the clock, watchful and attentive, keeping Ari at home as if he were still in the hospital. I said yes, not realizing what that would actually mean, grateful and relieved when she finally signed the release papers.

Once we returned home, I discovered that Ari was unable to hear or see me as the mother he'd come to know. It's as if my beloved son had left his body, to be replaced by a strange man on a rampage, one untrusting of the world, and of me. Until, that is, the medication turned that young man into a listless, groggy shadow of his former self, sleeping much of the day away. One afternoon Ari was sitting quietly at the dining room table and staring at his hands.

"What are you looking at?" I asked as I passed by, noting how he was turning his hands over slowly to see the back of them, then over again to study his palms.

"I am looking at the energy coming from my hands" Ari said. Look how beautiful it is," opening and closing his fingers as he continued to stare at them.

It was the first time I began to question the nature of psychosis, and whether some perceptions are actually based in reality, not entirely the hallucinations of an ill mind.

His father and I took turns being at home with him, in order to assure his safety and protection. At night I would keep an ear attuned to the sounds coming from his bedroom, sleeping only when I was certain that he was asleep. In the day I would hold office hours and meetings online, leaving only when I had to teach a class. When he was awake I would listen to his ranting, and lie to him when he'd ask what happened to the car keys. Weeks went by like that, and then melted into months, until the time came for him to begin his freshman year of college. Hopeful, yet ignorant, believing he was recovered, we sent him off and wished him well. Two months later he was back at home, entirely manic, unable to read or to think clearly. I had to teach my classes, and his father had to work, so when one of us could not stay at home with him, we'd take our son along to work. With his dad that meant riding in the passenger seat of the pickup truck he used for his landscaping business. With me it meant going to the university, and Ari waiting alone in my office while I taught class. One day, as Ari and I were walking across the university grounds, he inquired,

"I am embarrassing you, aren't I?"

"Of course not," I said, but I'd lied wanting not to shame him. There's something about the manic-psychotic state that attunes my son to the true emotional state of those who are around him. As such, he will say things no one else will say, going far past social taboos.

It took a few more years of life's tough lessons, but eventually, I learned not to lie to my son under any circumstances. Because lying was never helpful, no matter my good intentions, since every nuance of my voice and even that, which was not said, were apparent to him when in a hyper-perceptive, manic state.

Eventually Ari stabilized, for a while at least. He returned to college and I continued to live my dutiful life as a professor, a wife, a daughter, and mother. Through it all, our diligent daughter Kaya was hard at work and excelling in her high school classes. I tried to believe that our son was doing just fine being away from home. I continued to attend Quaker Meeting for worship, and practiced daily prayers and meditation. And I determined to not be beaten by life's jolts, wholly ignorant at that time of the toll mental illness can take on its victim, and on the family. I believed that if I was vigilant, the illness would eventually leave my son, so he could return to pursuit of the bright future life had promised. The weeks and months went by that way, and by November Ari returned home from college, manic and psychotic again. Life continued its tussle with me but I would not be defeated. I would not lose my son, or my hope.

We converted our cottage into a bed & breakfast rental, and I moved my office into the basement of our home. There were no windows down there as it was entirely underground. But it was quiet and conducive to concentration. One evening when I was working at my desk, Ari came down asking what I was doing.

"I'm writing a novel," I told him.

"One day you'll be writing about me," he replied.

From Rumi's *Desire and the Importance of Failing*:

Whatever that Presence gives us
we take in. Earth signs feed.
Water signs wash and freshen.
Air signs clear the atmosphere.
Fire signs jiggle the skillet,
so we cook without getting burnt.
And the Holy Spirit helps with everything,
like a young man trying to support a family.
We, like the man's young wife, stay home,
taking care of the house, nursing the children.
Spirit and matter work together like this,
in a division of labor.

Spring arrived, and with it a call from the human resources professional for an international study abroad program. Three weeks later I'd accepted their offer for the position of vice president, and walked away from my university appointment. It was a challenging position. The organization was financially strapped and threatened by the potential loss of its academic sponsor. I was willing to work hard and to do all I could to help because I believed in its mission. On the day before I was to leave on a work-related trip to Egypt, I got into an uncontrollable coughing fit. I continued to hack throughout the night, sometimes feeling that I was chocking. Early the next morning, on the same day of my scheduled international flight, I went to see a physician about the cough.

"I don't know what the problem is," he said after his examination.

I asked and he agreed to take an x-ray

"Unpack your bags," the doctor said when he returned to the examination room with the results. "You're not going anywhere."

The problem was a grossly enlarged thyroid, which on its left side had grown to over six inches. It was hidden behind my sternum, out of palpable detection, and had thus eluded an annual thyroid check. That growth was crushing my trachea making it hard for me to breath. Surgery was required, and urgently.

The appointment was scheduled and soon thereafter I purchased an audiotape of guided meditations, specifically for use in preparing for surgery. At night on my way to sleep, I'd listen to that tape, hoping it would help me to be less fearful. I'd never had surgery before. During one of these sessions, in a deeply meditative state, I observed my thyroid's injurious state. I acknowledged the role it had played in the growth and maturation of my body. And thanked it for helping to regulate my body functions, steadily releasing hormones into my blood. I was grateful but I was also aware: The gross enlargement of this organ was of my own making, an energetic expansion of all that I needed to say, but had not said. Believing myself to be a goodly, spiritual, loving person, for years I'd abstained from saying anything that I believed would be offensive or injurious to someone else. Rather than speaking my authentic truth to my husband, parents, children, employers, and others, I'd said what I thought people wanted to hear; I'd sought approval rather than to express with clarity my own needs; I choked back my words until the unspoken truth took its own ugly form, and began to choke me.

Early on the morning of the surgery, as I lay in the cold preparation room, the anesthesiologist asked if I had any questions. I had none, but wanted her to know that I was afraid of being put to sleep, and never waking up. She acknowledged my fear as being rational, agreeing that anesthesia is serious and risky. As the drip began I made a promise to myself. Never again would I refrain from saying what needed to be said; I would find and use my authentic voice in loving care of me.

I went under quickly.

Three hours later I awoke from the procedure, greatly relieved. This was my chance for a new beginning, for a different kind of relationship with my life, to rediscover and embrace my very own body in the wholeness of myself. But it wasn't for another six months, another manic-psychotic break for Ari, and the end of my marriage, that I truly committed to the care of myself. Divorce was an important step for my personal growth, but it would mean letting go of a deeply satisfying family life, the land and home I had come to cherish.

It was an amicable divorce, though very sad. As far as who would be leaving the property, my husband or me, I could not afford to "buy him out" of the value of the house, cottage, and land. I had no need for the barn and no knowledge of how to bush-hog the fields; he did. I was the one to have to go. Not wanting to disturb the children's living arrangements, or their sense of home, we decided that our son and daughter would stay in the home with their father. The entire occurrence was surreal to me. I left, taking with me only personal belongings and clothing. I left the place that truly and deeply felt like home; where I'd expected to spend the rest of my life, and had imagined future grandchildren would come to visit. I left; doing my best to disconnect from my husband of thirty years, the one person I knew truly saw me as me. I drove away from a young-adult son and teenage daughter; two people I loved more deeply than I have ever loved anyone. Returning to Rumi's *Desire and the Importance of Failing*, the poem continues:

> *God fixes a passionate desire in you,*
> *and then disappoints you.*
> *God does that a hundred times!*
> *God breaks the wings of one intention*
> *and then gives you another,*
> *cuts the rope of contriving,*
> *so you'll remember your dependence.*
> *But sometimes your plans work out!*
> *You feel fulfilled and in control.*
> *That's because, if you were always failing,*
> *you might give up. But remember,*
> *it is by failures that lovers*
> *stay aware of how they are loved.*
> *Failure is the key*
> *to the kingdom within.*

If failure was truly the key, then I was about to enter the kingdom within, of which Rumi had written. Enshrouded with a profound sense of having failed my family, my husband, and myself, I moved back to town.

I'd never lived alone. I'd resided with my parents until I finished high school, and then in the dorms with roommates. My college sweetheart and I moved into an apartment together during my senior year of college and two years later, we married.

That marriage lasted for thirty years, which means that until I was fifty-two years old I'd never slept alone in my own dwelling place. My new condo made for a wonderful home. But at night, when I fell asleep, the loneliness could sometimes overwhelm me. I had grown accustomed to curling up into a "spoon" with my arms around my husband's waist, and my belly against his back. I was used to the sound of his breathing, and the warmth of his skin against mine. I had come to like the comforting sense of having someone near when I was in the depths of dreaming, especially when I had nightmares and he'd hear me whimpering, and touch me gently until I quieted. And in the morning, it was always lovely if his eyes were open and smiling at me. I'd been glad to have him there with me, and perhaps had taken that for granted.

I did okay somehow, took pride in my independence, and the capacity to manage my affairs. To stave off loneliness, I purchased six orchids and placed them on the shelf of an eastern facing window. I remembered the teaching about plants, given by the Metepenagiag Mi'kmaq Nation visitor to the school. So one of the first things I would do each morning before leaving for work was to address to those lovely orchids, telling them how much I appreciated them. And I meant it; they were my companions, the only other living beings there with me. For over a year those orchids were prolific bloomers, stunningly beautiful. And I did cherish them.

My work life in the international program job took a horrifying turn, and I became preoccupied. Then my son had another, beastly manic break, seeing and hearing and feeling people and entities no one else could sense, angry and frustrated over the life that was slipping from his grasp. His doctor named it a delusional psychotic state, and increased the medication dosages. Meanwhile his friends were moving on, pursuing their college careers, and enjoying their social lives. I didn't know how to understand what was happening to him. What I did know is that I wanted him near to me, so my son came to stay with me for a few days each week. I began to lose myself to fear of losing him. None of the orchids bloomed that year, and two died.

Rumi ends his poem with the lines:

"Your prayer should be,
Break the legs of what I want to happen.
Humiliate my desire. Eat me like candy.
It's spring and finally I have no will."

V

Preparations for a Blessed Union

SOME PEOPLE ARE MORE than content to live alone. For me, the solitude quickly lost its allure, and I became sad. One evening after I'd retired to bed for the night, laying in the darkness, eyes open and wide awake, the reality of my situation loomed over me: I was 52 years old and single. My mind drifted to friends, who were my age and had divorced long before, but remained single still. I wondered if I would become like them; people who had loving hearts, but with no companions with whom to share their lives.

I turned to gaze out of the plate glass window, over the rooftops illuminated by the street lamps below. Sadness sunk into my chest. Feeling vulnerable and insecure, I tried to stop myself from heading down a path of self-doubt, questioning my worthiness. Curling myself into the fetal position I wept until I fell asleep.

When morning came I got myself up, showered, dressed, ate breakfast, and then took time for a brief meditation before heading to work. I sat on the designated cushion, lit a candle and closed my eyes. I observed the movement of my breath while silently repeating a mantra, which translated simply means, "I am that." It was only a moment before I settled into a quiet, inward state. That serenity turned into agitation.

"How could this be?" I wanted to know.

I had lost my cherished family life and my home. Ari was still sick with no indications of ever improving. My former husband was already seemingly happily partnered. Why did I have to be alone? I felt myself begin to sob, shoulders and abdomen shaking as I tried to catch my breath. And then, as if I were the observer, rather than the one involved, I heard myself yelling out loud, specifically addressing God:

"I want a new man in my life!" I shouted. "Someone who will see me for who I am, and love just me just as I am; someone who I can meditate with, and who will dance with me, and travel with me, and hold me when I am afraid. I want a handsome man who loves nature, and is honest and caring, and knows exactly who he is as a man. And he needs to be a good lover, and someone who likes to dance." I bellowed at the top of my voice: *"That's what I want!"*

Calming myself I rose to my feet, and walked quietly into the bathroom to wash the tears from my face. The tantrum had been cathartic and I felt exhausted yet refreshed. I picked up my bag and stepped out into the sunlit day, heading to the place of my employment.

That night, after a long day at work, something that I like to believe is the "still small voice" (of that which guides me), led me to my computer and an online dating service. I'd let my account with that service expire months before, but it was an easy process to restore that account. I reset my parameters for geographic location, age range, educational level, religious preferences, and race: Within 150 miles vicinity of my city; between the ages of 45 and 65; college educated; spiritual but not necessarily religious; no preference as to national origin or race.

Lots of men turned up as matches, but most of them were familiar from the last time I'd been on the site. The person who caught my eye immediately was one I'd not seen before, whose tagline read, "I'm Not Dead Yet!" as quoted from Monty Python. Something about his photo drew me in. His smile was compelling. But judging by his listed preferences, I wasn't going to be a very good match. For one, I lived much further away then he'd preferred. I also made less money, and I wasn't white. He listed as favorites some musicians I have never liked, and camping as an activity, which I had not yet come to enjoy. For some reason I ignored those mismatches, and read on, to the statement at the bottom of his profile where he'd written:

"Besides the earthy joys of being in nature, I am drawn to the life of the spirit, be it through meditation or music or poetry. I love to dance, with a partner who is free enough to just feel the music and not worry too much about the steps."

Right then I sent him a message, hoping he'd read my posting and then respond. My tag line read, "The Tao is dark and unfathomable. How does it make her radiant? Because she lets it." If that didn't scare him away, then maybe this was the one I'd asked for during my meditation earlier that day.

A reply came the following morning. His name was Bill.

Bill and I spoke by phone the next night and the following, then arranging to meet in person. For my sense of safety, our meeting place had to be in public, and during the daylight hours. We chose the apple harvest festival at Graves Mountain Lodge in Madison County, located midway between where he lived in Washington, DC, and my home in Charlottesville, Virginia. When that day arrived, I joyfully prepared kale chips to contribute to our picnic lunch. But on the drive there I grew increasingly anxious. I hadn't anticipated the heavy traffic, or the lack of cell phone service in that mountainous area. When finally I arrived, nearly thirty minutes late, there were hundreds of cars parked in the fields, and perhaps over a thousand people roaming around. I drove along the road toward where we'd agreed to meet, not knowing where or if I might find Bill. As my car slowly climbed the hill towards the mountain lodge, a man came walking in my direction. When we were near enough to be recognized from our photos, that man smiled broadly at me, and I at him.

"How in the world did you know I had arrived?" I asked rolling my window down. His timing was perfect.

"I'd been sitting on that porch for a while," he said pointing up to the lodge on the hill, "waiting there for you. I just got the feeling I should get up and walk this way," he exclaimed.

We spread a blanket out on the ground by the river and shared a meal. Afterwards we sat on a boulder in the river, our bare feet in the cold water as children splashed and played nearby. We talked about our recently ended, long-term marriages, described our children and explained the nature of our respective jobs. On raising the subject of how we first connected, I learned that Bill had renewed his listing on the online dating site at around the same time I'd renewed mine. So another way to tell this story is to say: I felt my loneliness, and deep desire for a companion. With all my heart I'd told God what I wanted. It was on the very next night that Bill and I found each other.

This same story could also be told as an allegory, in describing something that happened to me when I was on the island of Nantucket. It was during the busy tourist season, and I was trying to cross a street with very heavy and constant traffic flow. Standing on the sidewalk at a place where three roads intersect,

I watched the moving cars as they whizzed by. My thought was, "I'll never be able to get across." As soon as I realized the negative proclamation I'd made, I caught myself and remembered what I actually believe: *I will be well if I remain positive, have faith, and ask for exactly what I need.*

"Please help me cross the road," I whispered.

Immediately a car stopped, and the driver waved me on. The traffic on the other side of the road stopped as well.

After spending a great deal more time together, Bill and I took a trip to Martha's Vineyard, Massachusetts. While there I had an odd feeling, a somewhat troubling awareness that within the next year or two, I'd be going through some kind of personal transformation. Something was going to change me, though I did not know what that change would entail, or what to expect as a result. Whatever it was, it would be beyond my control; it had to happen and would involve a difficult process.

I shared that hunch with Bill over dinner at a restaurant one night. He listened quietly as I tried my best to explain. After our meal he took my hand as we walked along the shore, back to the cottage we'd rented. What I remember about that evening is how bright the moon was, reflecting on the calm waters of the Vineyard Sound. I also remember Bill's response to what I'd told him as we'd settled in that night to sleep.

"Whatever it is that you are about to go through, I want to be able to be there for you; but to be there for you, I need to be your husband."

His proposal rendered me nearly speechless, so it wasn't until the next morning when he'd asked again, that I gave a clear reply.

A Unity minister couple would marry Bill and me the following spring. Unity had come a long way since my early days in the church, and we felt well supported by them in our prenuptial counseling and planning. We attended one of their Sunday services to be certain we'd made the right decision. It felt just right to us being there, in their beautiful sanctuary, under the leadership of the ministerial couple . . . though neither of us was inclined to actually start attending Unity, or the services of any religious institution, for that matter. Bill had spent his youth and over twenty years as an adult with the United Church of Christ. Since our coming together, he had switched to spending Sunday mornings hiking in the woods, alone. The foothills of the Blue Ridge Mountains had become his church. And when I could get there, any redwood forest, or the ocean, had become mine.

The wedding plans had been laid, and the guest list confirmed. But there was still something I had to do before we could be wed.

Where the knowledge came from I can't say. But I've known this for a while: sexual intercourse leaves an energetic trail, a thread of continued fastening between the people involved. If we could see what actually is, there would be billions of streams of cloud-like substances, some murky, others bright, crisscrossing the world from one person to another. Some of us would have just one or a few of those, while others would have many, many such energetic lines of connection. Some of those lines would be very thin, and others much thicker. If we could feel into those lines, and use our bodies to sense them, we'd have a vague notion of still being attached to those people with whom we've had sex. Some of these connections would be barely perceptible. Others would be quite strong. It doesn't matter how long it's been, but rather depends on the intention behind the sexual encounters, the state of completion of the purpose, and our authentic desire and capacity for letting go. It also depends on how strongly one person is working to draw energy from another through those connecting threads.

It didn't occur to me until my thirty-year marriage had nearly ended that I'd been tapped by the energetic pulls of other men. I am not speaking of merely emotional attachments. This is something else, although emotions can strengthen those cords. We assume that copulation is a purely physical act. But as I have come to more clearly understand from the mare named Beauty and the stallion named Juano (I will explain this further in Part II), for horses and humans too, sex is much more than that.

I wanted to prepare myself for a sacred union with Bill. By the word "sacred" I mean that our marriage would bring connection of body, and of mind, and also of spirit, as supported by the Inner Light (using Quaker parlance, the Inner Light refers to the divine presence of the human soul). I would find a way to remove the energetic attachments of others, in order to make myself entirely and wholly available for loving my husband. Immersing myself in living water would have to be part of that process. And I knew just where to find that. Other than that, I needed to ask for the guidance of Spirit on what further to do.

When I shared my plans for a pre-marital cleansing ritual my Jewish women friends all said, "Oh, a Mikvah!" Jewish tradition uses a variety of water rituals and blessings, one being for women to cleanse themselves after menstruation. I'd never heard of a Mikvah, but I did know of baptismal uses of water in Christianity, of ritual ablutions in Islam, and in Japanese Buddhism. I'd also read Masaru Emoto's writing on the capacity of water to respond to our thoughts. I knew from my intentional visits to various thermal pools in Costa Rica, Ecuador, and Virginia that living, flowing water can absorb and remove elements of emotion and energy attached to us, those that no longer serve us, and that we no longer need.

I was delighted when the woman minister from Unity accepted my invitation to come along on the trip to the Jefferson Pools at Warm Springs, Virginia. Twelve other women participated including my mother, sisters, sister-in-law, daughter, and friends.

I prepared beforehand by writing in a journal. There, I listed by name each person I'd encountered sexually in my life, reflected on my memories of those encounters, and then adapted a prayer of release for each:

> *"Spirit of Life, Source of my being:*
>
> *"I ask for healing and release from energies I no longer need or wish to hold in attachment.*
>
> *"I see in my mind's eye* (name of person) *standing before me, and I ask* (name of person) *to forgive me. I take full responsibility for all the pain I have caused you in this life and all lives and times back to the very beginning of time, known and unknown. I forgive you all the pain you have caused me. And I forgive myself.*
>
> *"I ask that the root, cause, core, effects, and every hair and tittle of this energy be transmuted and removed from my being and aura forever.*
>
> *"From my heart I send pure love. I see it flowing into my crown chakra, and out of my heart, to* (name of person), *surrounding them and filling them completely.*
>
> *"I let go and release* (name of person) *into their rightful place in the divine plan of life.*
>
> *"Thank you, Divine Spirit, Source of my being, which guides and supports me.*
>
> *"And so it is."*

We began our outing to the thermal springs with a circle of the women, gathered in the home of my friend Janet, a trainer and healing practitioner who is well versed in guiding such endeavors. I explained my intention and purpose for the trip to the baths. Each woman then offered her blessing with a personal message for me. We boarded the fifteen-passenger coach I'd hired for the nearly two-hour ride into the Shenandoah Mountains. I'd asked my fellow travelers to refrain from talking for the duration of the ride, and during the soak as well, so that I could continue to journal and recite the prayers I'd written, in the sacred space of meditative silence. They were happy to oblige, and each woman, it seemed to me, used the time for her own reflective purposes.

It was late morning when we arrived at the Jefferson Pools, a bright blue-skied, sunny day at the end of May, two days before the actual marriage ceremony. A couple was inside, already soaking when we got there. Otherwise we had the warm hexagonal thermal pool all to ourselves. Quietly, without speaking, our group entered by the wooden steps. The water, about five feet deep, bubbled up from underground. Crystal clear, it had a faintly green hue from the high mineral content, and could be heard flowing from inside, out into the running stream below. The property includes the Warm Springs Bath Houses historic structures, (one for women and one for men), which provide (unheated) shelter from the elements. The domed wooden roof has gaps and spaces between the painted white boards, so while floating on one's back, you can see patches of sky above, and on rainy days, occasionally feel cool drops of water on your bare skin. The buildings show their age: over two hundred and fifty years, circa 1761.

The first thing that I did on entering the pool was to thank the spirit of the water for its healing properties. I expressed my intentions and purpose on being there, and asked the water to carry away from me the energetic remnants of my past lovers. Slowly, one by one, I recalled the man I had been with. Saying his name, silently, I then recited the prayer of karmic release I had written in the journal. After the prayer had been uttered, I submersed my body under the water, three times. Between each I would clear my mind by floating on my back, while listening to the sound of my breath, which is particularly audible with ears underneath water. When I had finished with releasing each person on my list, I asked Spirit if there was anything more I'd left to do in the purification process. Thinking I'd finished my list I rested, my mind empty and quiet, my arms draped over a floatation tube.

After a few moments, my serene state was interrupted, sensing the presence of a high school friend; someone I'd not seen in forty years, a person who had died unexpectedly only a few months before. Her soul was ready to leave, to move on from this world.

"Release me too," I heard her say.

It had been a very long time since she and I had been together; I was a young teen then. But indeed, she and I had messed around on sleepover, experimenting in discovery of our sexuality.

"Could this actually be?" I asked myself, "That she and I had stayed connected in that way?"

I spoke her name in the prayer of karmic release, sent her my love and asked her forgiveness. Then I forgave myself. A sense of peace came over me and at that point, I knew the process was done.

When my friend Janet sensed that completion, she gathered the other women around me, everyone with a hand touching my skin underneath my legs, back, and head, keeping me afloat, my mother taking hold of a foot. Together, in that gathering of joy, we all celebrated my unencumbered state.

Now I was truly ready to say, "I do."

VI

This is My Son, and He Pleases Me

BILL WAS AWARE OF bipolar disorder because of its incidence in his family. But he had never encountered the kind of psychosis it presented in my son's condition. He vowed early in our relationship to support me, observing the exacting demands it had on my life. He also noted, often to my deaf ears, the ways in which I'd allowed my son's condition to consume me. I'd vowed to be there for him through sickness and health, because of my love for him, and he was my son.

Our society tends to shun, stigmatize, and render invisible those people who have mental illnesses. Many people seem purposely to avoid direct contact with them, or at best, to notice but quickly judge, devaluing them as lesser beings. For many it's apparently still taboo to speak with those outside the family, or to speak at all, about afflicted family members; that would bring embarrassment and shame. Those who have no experience with mental illness are at a loss for what to say to those of us who do. Awkwardness often thus ensues in social situations.

Wanting to do what's best, and sometimes just wanting a break, we send our afflicted loved ones to institutions, isolated from the rest of society, to be medicated, silenced, and subdued.

Here's what I have come to believe: sometimes those with mental illness see and speak truths the rest of us are unwilling to accept. Often it's not them we are shunning, but more so ourselves. It's not them we fear, but our own loose hold on what we consider to be reality. There have been times when my son seems saner than me. There are moments during Ari's psychotic episodes, and when I realize he is attuned to other realities, seeing beings that the rest of us cannot see. He crosses dimensions of time and space, hearing voices the rest of us cannot hear. That's not to say he should go without treatment; in wishing to be socially connected, personally fulfilled, and gainfully employed in our society he is left with no other choice. Medicine can be a very good thing.

After seven years of rapid cycling, manic psychotic episodes, my son took on the appearance of a deranged homeless man. His clothes were often unchanged, dirty, and smelling, and he gave little attention to his appearance. Sometimes I would have to wonder, "Who is this person?" Often talking out loud to people in his head, I grew embarrassed to be with him and shuddered to be with him in public. Until the day that something shifted in me.

I was waiting for him inside of a restaurant where we regularly met. I saw him outside, through the plate glass window, mumbling and smiling, as if in response to something someone had said, someone no one else could see. I watched him, and was moved by an incredible love, a love more magnificent than any I'd ever felt, welling up in my heart and expanding. *This is my son*, I thought, not with shame but with gratitude and awe, even pride. I saw his strength and his endurance, and also his complete and utter freedom. I saw him as the brilliant artist he is. There he was, Ari; my beautiful son, named after the Greek

Aristotle meaning, "one seeking the highest good." The same son who came to me in a dream a few days after my daughter Zoe's death saying, "Don't be sad, Mommy. I'm coming soon." This son of mine would become one of my greatest teachers.

After our meal, as Ari and I walked the bricked-over Main Street of what is called "the downtown mall," I took note of the people we passed, especially those with apparent mental challenges and disabilities. Strangely so, as if I was seeing them for the first time, there was nothing about any of them that was off-putting. In fact, they became to my eyes a rich and integral part of the landscape of our larger community. The man, who walks up and down the mall shouting "nonsense" at the top of his voice and clapping loudly, needn't be silenced. Nor the man clothed in tattered pants and shirt that do not fit him, who waves his arms wildly in announcing to the world, through song, his wayward need not be made invisible. Instead, what I saw that day and have seen every day since, is just how interconnected we all are, no matter our mental state.

Between February and May of that year, Ari improved significantly. Indeed, to my weary heart and exhausted mind, my son seemed completely back to normal. I'd been given a prayer by my godmother, directed to Ari's wellness, and had recited it twice a day for that entire time. His father and I followed intuition and had taken a risk, moving Ari into his own apartment. He continued to improve. I continued to pray: Come forth to Ari Berne, Ye Angels of the Lord; May the choir of Angels receive him and guide him into perpetual light. By June, Ari appeared to have recovered.

Believing my son was finally well I relaxed, let down my emotional guard, and celebrated his wellbeing. A few weeks later Ari and I took a walk along the same pedestrian mall of our city where he and I have often walked. Increasingly, as we proceeded Ari talked psychotically. Witnessing his mind slipping back to illness, I lost my equilibrium. I grew agitated and told him to stop talking that way. Ari turned to me and questioned whether I actually even loved him.

In a sudden explosion of anger I screamed an expletive and told him to get away from me. I was losing control, and totally out of character began to shout out loud in fury to the God who had misled me to believe that Ari, my precious son, was healed and would be all right after all. The daily prayers and candle lighting had not worked. Despite my spiritual vigilance and faith, I determined that God had not done anything to help my son. Despite Ari's complete compliance with psychotherapy visits, and regularly taking his medications, nothing was working and he was obviously not getting any better. I threw myself against the brick wall of a building, pounding my fist against it. Shouting from rage, and losing my faith and belief in God, I also lost a grip on my own mind.

Ari left the mall to walk home. I headed for my car, somewhat delirious. As I turned the corner, onto the side street where my car was parked, a man sitting on a nearby bench who was clearly looking at me, raised his hand to get my attention.

"Hi! How are you today?" he asked.

I did my best to utter some kind of polite response to this cordial person who was a complete stranger to me. But I was not feeling well; all I did was wave back in his direction. I got into the car and slowly began to drive away, passing right by the man who had spoken. It was a very hot day, and having rolled my car window down, I heard that man clearly as I drove by. He had turned his body so as to face me directly, leaned toward my open window, saying, "You take care now, and be careful driving so that you can get home safe okay?" Hearing that brought me back to my senses, and to tears.

This man was not as he appeared. Whoever or whatever he was, he was there just exactly when I needed help. The feeling I had as he spoke was the same feeling I had the day I was late for my medical appointment, when told that an unidentified mysterious man arrived before me to let the nurses know that I was running late. As I drove away, in a much calmer state, I began to suspect that I'd just had an encounter with God. I drove passed Ari walking home and offered him a ride. He, in turn, offered to take me to the hospital for a psychiatric evaluation.

"You've been there for me when I needed help. Let me be here for you this time," he pleaded.

I'd scared my son with my explosive behavior, but it was he who stayed strong this time. I reassured him that I would be okay, and promised him I'd call my therapist (someone I had seen on and off over the years since Zoe's death) as soon as I got home. I made that call and left a message asking for her help. She returned that call right away. After I explained to her what had transpired, she reminded me that whenever Ari has gone into a psychotic state, he has always eventually stabilized.

Three weeks later, Ari and I were driving in my car. Suddenly he exploded yelling, "When are you going to stop this!"

"This" referring to my incessant worrying and fear, my meddling and anxiety about whether Ari is, or ever will be all right. He spoke with such wisdom and clarity, not at all as someone who is mentally ill. He spoke as a self-aware, frustrated son deploring his mother for sneaking around and spying on him— seeking to determine whether he took his medications; whether he'd done his laundry and cleaned his dishes; where he has been, and whether he has gotten enough sleep.

"Don't you have your own dreams you want to pursue?" he questioned. "Ask yourself what you need to do, for you!"

Then he told me how grateful he was for all I have done to take care of and to support him, but that now it's time for me to let go, and to get on with pursuing my own personal aspirations.

There must have been a painful expression on my face.

"I'm not suffering," he said. "And anyway, you can't do this for me. I am the one who has to sort out how to manage this disorder."

"You are still my responsibility and I care about you," I reproached

"Why don't you live your own life and stop caring so much about mine?" he asked.

"But you are my son," I spoke softly.

"I was born through you this time as your son, but I don't belong to you," he continued.

I thought of the time, back when I was a rebellious teen, desperate for a sense of independence. I'd written onto a piece of paper and placed on my mother's pillow, the words of a poem by Khalil Gibran, "On Children," which begins:

> Your children are not your children.
> They are the sons and daughters of Life's longing for itself.
> They come through you but not from you,
> And though they are with you yet they belong not to you.
> You may give them your love but not your thoughts,
> For they have their own thoughts.
> You may house their bodies but not their souls,
>
> for their souls dwell in the house of tomorrow,
> which you cannot visit, not even in your dreams.

I thought of that and wondered how my mother was able to let go of me. Perhaps it was because I was mentally healthy, physically able, and exhibited the capacity to take care of myself. *Ari is different*, I affirmed to myself. *I already let go of my daughter to grow in her independence, but I can't let Ari go in that way because of his illness. If I do, he might fall into terrible tragedy.*

Ari was quiet for a moment and then continued,

"You might be my mother in this life, but you might not have been before, and might not be in the next. We are all alone you know; we come in alone, we are here alone, and we'll leave that way, too. We each have to figure out how to live our lives. So please, please, stop worrying about me so that I can live mine."

My breathing shifted from constricted and shallow to flowing and eased, as I moved into trusting acceptance. Yes, indeed I had my own personal dreams and aspirations. There were definitely things I still wanted to do.

When August arrived Ari, my daughter Kaya, and their father went to Cape Cod for vacation, to the same family beach house we had visited annually as a family since the children were born. During that same time, Bill and I went to a lake in New Hampshire, where since our meeting we'd rented a cabin in the woods. Tom, a friend from high school I'd recently reconnected with, came to stay with us at the cabin for a day and night, bringing along his companion, Choong. A bond of new friendship with her formed quickly, and for many weeks following Choong and I spoke by phone and met together remotely for meditation practices. Choong worked with light energy and also with Mother Mary and the Christ, in doing healing work with Ari and with me. Her purpose, as she explained it, was to free us both to expand into our higher Christ selves, as supported by universal love.

Later that fall, my husband and I were in Italy visiting friends who live in the countryside above the town of Assisi, Italy. While there I attended a small-group meditation in the home of a local farmer's wife. A woman named Roseanna, a yoga teacher and also a gifted healer, led a session for a group of three other women and me. At the end of an hour, Roseanna encouraged us to share any images we had during her guided meditation. I'd seen a woman, in her late 20s perhaps. She was beautiful with dark shoulder-length hair and an olive complexion. I did not recognize who she was but was happy to see her. I wanted to share this image with the group but instead I began to weep. In Italian, Roseanna asked what my emotions were about. My friend translated for us.

"I think it's about my son," I said. "He has a mental illness and is not well."

Roseanne approached me and touched my chest, her hand over my heart. Then she touched my head. More sobbing ensued and with it memories of my first-born child, the baby girl that we named Zoe. I shared that with the group.

"You never cut the umbilicus with her, your infant daughter who died," Roseanna explained. I understood that she meant that figuratively, not literally so.

"If you do that and release your daughter, then your son will get better. The problem is not your son being sick, but that you have confused him with her. You have to let her go now."

Zoe was born without a brain. Ari was born two years after her death. Could it actually be that I had emotionally and perhaps energetically been holding onto her all this time, and that Ari's been compromised as a result? Is it possible that the trauma of my daughter's gestation, birth, and death, left remnants in my womb that affected him? When Ari was about 7 years old, and Kaya 4, we told them about their sister Zoe, of her birth and death. I'd been lighting a candle every year on May 12th, her birthday, which I lit for the three days unit the 15ᵗʰ to memorialize her life. After explaining what had happened to Zoe Ari looked up with furrowed brow and rubbed his hand across his brow, anguish in his eyes.

"I feel like I was there, too," he said. His first tattoo, ten years later at age 17, was the name Zoe on his upper arm.

Roseanna offered to help me with Zoe, and to let her go. I was grateful for the offer and accepted it. The next morning we met again, this time in a room on the farm designated for healing work. As I lay on the massage table and Roseanna worked at my side, I realized that the image of a woman I had seen during meditation the day before, was what my daughter would likely look like today had she continued to live. Her age would be 28. After our session was done, and I'd followed Roseanna's instructions, I sensed Zoe moving into the distance as a freed spirit, farther and farther away.

Early in the evening after my session with Roseanna, walking the winding, stone streets of the ancient town of Assisi, Bill and I came upon a church built in 1539, and then renovated in Baroque style in the 17th century. I was drawn inside to find gold-painted Roman columns and crown moldings, and life-sized statues also painted gold. The walls were painted blue, as was the ceiling, which depicted angelic and other beings. The main figure in the imagery above the altar was the Madonna. Though I have never been of the Catholic faith, something came over me and I felt led to sit in meditation. Gazing on Mother Mary's statue form, I heard myself pray:

*Forgive me. I misunderstood; they are not mine. The children I
bore belong to you, the Great Mother of us all. I am giving them
back to you, releasing them from the grip of my possessive sense of
mothering, and from my inhibiting fears. Let them be free to be
what they were meant to be, and to fulfill the purpose of their own
souls. Please give me the strength to let them go, even as I continue
to love them.*

When I stood from the pew to walk out, I began to feel
woozy. Bill took my arm and we walked slowly to the back of
the church. I dropped onto the bench by the door, and tears
flowed. Something had moved deep inside of me.

Outside, as we made our way back onto the plaza, Bill
noticed a sign explaining that the Santa Maria Sopra Minerva
church was originally a temple to Minerva, the Roman goddess
of wisdom, built in the first century, BC.

Perhaps what I'd felt in there was the presence of the divine
feminine. Whatever that was, I'd was touched by grace that day.

PART TWO

VII

To Be Drawn In by What You Love

IN THE STATE BETWEEN awake and asleep, that limbo awareness of contrasting worlds, she comes to me. My senses adjust to perceive her equine form. It is a dream-like occurrence and yet my eyes are open. I am aware and fully conscious of her ethereal shape, which seems to be suspended just over my head. Morning light beckons me to rise, but the auspicious presence renders me supine. I remain still and relaxed.

"Is that really you?" I inquire.

The white streak from her forehead down her nose marks a striking contrast to the black bay of her coat. This is definitely Beauty, the mare. Through her dark, penetrating eyes, something mysterious is looking back at me.

"There's more for you to write," she conveys.

I attune my inward ear to the channel through which she speaks.

"More about what?" I return in the silence of our exchange. "Regarding horses?" I surmise, curious about how she is speaking to me. Beauty lives in Costa Rica. I am in my bedroom in Virginia.

"Not horses, humans," she relays. "Come back so I can help you to understand, and then you will know what to write."

Now I am fully awake. I smile at the seemingly absurd notion that this mare is offering to help me write another book.

"Alright then," I say in an audible whisper. "Soon. I will come back."

With that, Beauty's form fades away.

I notice the lavender color of our bedroom walls, and the pale green buds on the walnut tree that spreads its branches just beyond the windowpanes. I recall the last time I was with her, on my way to conduct a study abroad program. We were taking students by ship to ports of call throughout Central and South America, embarking from Costa Rica. I decided to first spend a few days with my friend Debbie at the Leaves and Lizards eco-retreat. One quiet day during my visit there, after all the other quests had checked out, Debbie offered to take me on an afternoon horseback ride. I was thrilled.

Ronald the stableman saddled up for us two of the resident mares: Beauty, who was offered to me, and Debbie's favorite horse, Gitana. Our ride began in an open pasture of tall grasses, hilly terrain but not too steep for me to handle comfortably. I was excited to be with my friend, and on horseback. Feeling relaxed and carefree, I took in the gorgeous scenery as we rode: the gumdrop green hills all around and in the distance, Lake Arenal, flanked by the volcano of the same name. Then without warning, in comic-book slow motion, I am sliding leftwards off the saddle. Calling out for Debbie, ahead of me by about 25 feet, she turns around just in time to watch me hit the ground.

Beauty's front hoof was about an inch from my face. My fear was that she would step on me with a thousand pounds of crushing weight. But the mare held herself still. Debbie dismounted Gitana, and led her horse in my direction.

"Are you alright, Rosa?" she asked, her nursing background apparent in her voice.

It was hard to speak, not because I was in pain or in shock, but because my focus was on the tall grasses blowing gently around me as they framed the sky in my view from the ground, and the puffy white clouds motionless in the wide cerulean expanse. The sweet air was light and pure. I felt fine, right where I was.

"Rosa?" she asked again. "Can you move?"

"I'm okay," I managed to say.

"Good, then get up," she urged.

Preferring to remain right there, I didn't budge. It was all so serene. And I was in awe, perceiving the world as an incredibly beautiful and precious place to be. Even the ground underneath me felt comfortable, cradle-like, as if offering me its support.

"Come on Rosa, get up," Debbie repeated, her face hovering above me, Gitana standing by her side. Debbie's forehead was furrowed, her tone more insistent. "You ride Gitana and I will take Beauty," she chuckled in a conciliatory offer.

Debbie must have been concerned, and she was being generous with me as Gitana was her favorite horse. I continued to lie there, silently taking in the perfection of the world.

"Let's go," Debbie insisted, as she extended her hand toward me.

"Why rush?" I wondered. "Everything is so lovely from right here where I am," I thought but did not say.

Debbie's concern, she told me later, was the possibility of venomous snakes in the grass.

It took another moment but I did finally accept her hand, and Debbie brought me to my feet.

"Do you want to go back?" she asked. "We can skip the ride and do something else."

"Nope," I returned, placing my foot into the stirrup and hoisting myself up into the saddle on Gitana's back. "I don't need to go back." Though I did feel a minor pain in my head, and I was somewhat lightheaded. "Let's go," I said. "I'm fine."

We rode for the rest of the afternoon, over hillsides, across farmland, past many herds of cattle, through the forests, and over two rivers and many streams. We greeted residents of the tiny villages as we passed through them, and took in the sounds of primates and birds that were active in the trees. At the second river we stopped to let the horses rest and drink. The water break for horses quickly turned into their play stop, with me joining in, Gitana and I splashing water at each other, she using her front hoof and me using my hand, me soaking wet in my clothing and laughing for joy.

At the end of the day, Debbie and I said our farewells. My bags were packed and I was ready for the nearly four-hour car ride to San Jose. But I hardly noticed that time pass. I felt a profound shift in my state of consciousness, looking out on the world around me with heightened sensory awareness and an indescribable sense of peace. On arriving at the hotel where the study abroad faculty and staff were convening, someone looked at me and said, "Wow! Your eyes; you look like someone who has become enlightened!" Maybe so. For that day at least, that's exactly how it felt.

I lay in bed musing over what had happened on that afternoon ride, and that very morning with Beauty, until the sound of the grinder in the kitchen downstairs ended my reverie. Soon the aroma of fresh-brewed coffee would waft through the air. What an enticing smell, even to me as one who does not drink it. It was time to get up and turn my attention to the pile of student research papers on my desk in need of grading.

A few hours later the telephone rings.

"Hello?" I answer.

"Rosa?" I hear a voice ask. It's Debbie, calling from Costa Rica.

"Something strange is going on with Beauty," she announces. "When I was down in the barn this morning she kept staring at me. She seemed anxious as if she had something to tell me. She kept trying to get my attention. When I went to her she started nudging me. I don't know why but I think Beauty's behavior has something to do with you, Rosa."

"That's interesting," I reply.

"Do you have any idea of what's going on with her?" Debbie asks.

"Actually, I think I do," I say, explaining that most likely Beauty wants to be certain that I received her message.

"Please tell Beauty that I heard her," I instruct Debbie. "Let her know that I will come to her as soon I can."

That was early April, an intense time of the academic year. I was swamped with end-of-semester tasks such as preparing last lectures and writing the final exam. I knew that the soonest I could get to Costa Rica would be the end of May, after graduation; I vowed to go then. But when the semester came to a close I felt pressure to complete a book project long overdue to the publisher. And there was also the matter of preparing for my summer school classes. So instead of flying south to Costa Rica, at the end of May, I drove north into the foothills of the Blue Ridge Mountains, where I'd rented a cabin to use as a writing retreat. I hunkered down there for about three weeks and was very productive. By late June I'd completed the manuscript, and with that behind me, felt a tremendous sense of relief. It seemed like a good time for that visit with Beauty.

Except that my attention was diverted. A notice came into my university email account that student evaluations from spring semester were now available for review. Quite unexpectedly, I opened them to discover I'd received a below average rating! This had been a class of 350 freshman-engineering students. I knew it would be a challenge, as I'd never taught such a large lecture course before. But it never occurred to me that I would fail so miserably. What a shock. This was a first for me; in my twenty-five years of teaching I'd always received high ratings. The evaluations revealed a considerable amount of student discontent with the course, and with me! I took some particularly biting comments personally. Realizing what a debacle the course had been, melancholy soon took hold. I was devastated.

"What were your goals for the course?' my son Ari asked me when I told him about the student reviews. Having been enrolled in large lecture courses at another university, he had a student's perspective.

"I wanted the students to reconsider their assumptions about the role of technology in the world, to look at some of the formidable challenges we have created in our technological hubris, and to be willing to take moral responsibility for their work as future professional engineers," I explained.

"And you expected them to *like* that?" he chuckled. "Go back and look again at the evaluations," he advised. "Find the kernels of truth in them. Use those to help you to approach the students differently next semester."

It was sage advice. But I was beyond consoling. It felt as if a chemical was seeping into my brain, and fighting against it was of no use. A depression was looming. My son could see it in my eyes.

"I know what to do to help you," Ari said. "Come with me. We'll take care of this. I have just the therapy you need." I felt completely helpless, as if losing control of my mental equilibrium. Unsure of what to expect I willingly followed my twenty-four year old son to his car.

We climbed inside of his minivan and he proceeded to connect an mp3 player to the car audio system. He selected a piece of heavy metal music, pressing "play." The sound was overwhelming, the car windows vibrating as the electronic screeches consumed the atmosphere, and me.

"Turn that off!" I demanded.

"No, listen to it," he insisted.

"But I don't want to," I returned, my voice rising to a near scream.

"Just listen," Ari calmly suggested.

"I am asking you to please turn that off," my voice faded to a whimper. "It makes me feel like crying." Ari reached for the controls and turned the music up louder.

"Let the music inside of you," he insisted. The harsh intensity of the electrified sounds makes me angry, and I tell him so. "Good, keep feeling it," he demanded. I was uncomfortable with the outrage that I sensed inside me. Finally I abandoned my defenses, shouting curse words until my voice went hoarse.

"Good job," my son offered calmly as he changed the musical selection to a more subdued beat. "Now I want you to see yourself standing in the lecture hall with those same 350 students. Feel and remember what a great professor you are."

Listening to the music he had selected, I visualized the scene. The tightness released from my chest, and my breathing eased.

"Thank you, Ari." I exclaimed. "I feel much better now."

That night I fall into a very deep sleep, emotionally drained and exhausted. But in the morning I awake feeling completely myself, refreshed. The sense of utter shame has left me. Amazingly, the melancholy has also gone. I realize what I need to do. In addition to teaching the summer school course I have already committed to, I focus my summer's efforts on redesigning the unsuccessful course in preparation for teaching it again in the fall. In absorbing myself in both tasks, going to be with Beauty slips entirely from my mind.

Time passes quickly and suddenly it is the end of September, a third of the way through fall semester at the university. I believe we were off to a good start with the revamped course, though I feel an unexplained dreariness and lack of motivation. Something was off-kilter, but I could not fathom what it was. Finally it dawned on me: five months had passed since I had awakened to her ethereal visit, and I had yet to go see Beauty.

On an early morning in mid-October, during "fall reading days," I set off for Costa Rica. I can only manage a brief trip, but at least I am going. The rising sun lights the Blue Ridge Mountains, the golden and auburn leaves the markings of autumn. Bundled up against the chill I make my way to the airport, sleep through the hour-long flight to Charlotte, and again for much of the connecting flight into San Jose. Arriving at Juan Santamaría International Airport, my friend Enrique is there to greet me. For the three-and-a-half hour drive north, over the mountains to the town of Monterrey, we enjoy a conversation about life, and loss, and love.

Though no one is there when we arrive late in the afternoon at the main office of the Leaves and Lizards Cabin Retreat, Enrique is able to find the key to Coco, my assigned cabin. The first thing I do after we unload is to sit in a rocking chair on the porch. The entire place is very quiet as it is off-season for tourists, and no one is in residence besides the owners, Debbie and her husband Steve, and me. It is wonderful to be here, yet disorienting. One day earlier I was in Virginia lecturing to 350 students in an auditorium. Now I find myself looking out over an expanse of tropical flora, with not a person in sight.

A tropical rainstorm threatens in the distance. The movement of warm, moist air brings the fragrances of frangipani and jasmine to my nose. Banana and papaya tree branches frame the porch. Ferns and paradise flowers grow lush on the ground below. A profusion of tropical greenery spreads out across the vast valley toward Arenal, the perfectly cone-shaped volcano, and its full majesty hidden beneath a suspended swirl of grey clouds, hovering over its crater. It too is quiet, dormant at least for now.

During earlier visits to Costa Rica, Arenal had been a source of inspiration for me. The first time I encountered it was during an active period of flowing lava. Standing about a football field away from its base, I'd heard the sound of its rhythmic off-gassing. It was as if the volcano were breathing. In tears, I dropped to the ground, sensing in Arenal's activity the fundamental "aliveness" of Earth.

I unpack my boots, blue jeans, and toiletries, leaving the rest in the suitcase since I am to be here only four nights. I then walk the rock-covered road that winds over the hillside to the barn. Most of the herd is here, but Beauty is the only horse I recognize, her distinctive features befitting her name: a black bay coat with a wide white streak running down her face. I pay my respects to her first, as she is the primary reason for my visit. I explain to her that it took me longer than I'd intended to get here, but that as she requested, I did come. Beauty doesn't display any particular acknowledgment of my presence, or of what I said. She just stands looking at me as any horse would, and for a moment I feel flustered, losing confidence in myself, and questioning my newfound capacity to understand horses. Before leaving the barn I greet the other horses with a simple stroke on the neck or a hello, and then return to the cabin to rest and settle in.

Heading back to the porch of Coco cabin, I recline in a swinging hammock, mesmerized by the volcano, until my fascination is broken by the sound of an engine, and of tires bumping along the rutted road heading in my direction. Shortly I hear it stop nearby, and a jeep door opening and closing.

"Rosa, are you here?" someone says.

I recognize Debbie's voice: opening the cabin door I find her standing there and smiling. It's so good to see her, and to be back at her Costa Rica home.

The horses that live and work here have been teachers for me, since my 2010 visit that led to *When the Horses Whisper*, about interspecies communication and the matrix of interconnected life in which humans, other animals, and plants are held. I have watched the herd work with disabled children; with adolescent victims of sexual abuse; and with weary, stressed-out adults whose overactive, high-pressure lives are taking a toll on their emotional and physical health. I've seen how compassionate, patient, and perceptive these horses can be in their therapeutic relationships with human beings.

"Debbie," I say sheepishly after we've greeted one another. "I need for you to re-introduce me to the herd. I went to the stable to see the horses but it's been so long that I didn't recognize any of them other than Beauty, of course."

Debbie rolls her eyes. Her glare incites my guilt about such forgetfulness. I've visited multiple times over the last four years, spending considerable time with the horses during my stays. "It's been nine months since I was here last," I remind her, "and I since then I have taught over 700 students. How am I supposed to keep all of your horses' names straight?" I argue in my own defense.

Early the next day, while eating breakfast in the dining hall, Debbie shows up saying, "Rosa, someone is here to see you."

"Really?" I ask, unable to imagine who that might be. I follow Debbie outside of the open-air dining hall. A golden-coat horse is standing there. He is looking directly at me.

"Hi Dorado!" I say, hoping that I have correctly identified him. I reach out to stroke his face.

"What a sweet boy you are to come see me."

Dorado gets straight to the point. And I hear him clearly:

Where have you been? Are you are going to stay here this time and work with us, or will you be leaving again?

His genuineness takes me aback. I stand there looking at Dorado, who is still looking straight into my eyes. I can't help but feel moved and I cannot resist him. Dorado wants to know of my willingness to truly be here. My reaction is tears and I turn away. Whoever said that horses live entirely in the present with no memory of the past or thought for the future got it wrong. Dorado is reminding me of my implicit promise to be connected and available as a part of the herd. The poet Rumi wrote,

"Allow yourself to be drawn in by what you love."

How can I resist? I do love Dorado and other horses in the herd, and yet I am conflicted over how to be with them as a sometimes visitor, to cultivate a genuine relationship; my life is with my loved ones back home.

I finish breakfast and head straight for the stable. Most of the horses are in the midst of their morning feeding, standing over the bins of hay, heads down and chewing. Titán, the gelding with whom I had my first horse communication is at the far end, standing just inside of the muddy corral. When he fails to acknowledge me when I call to him, I approach gingerly around the urine puddles and droppings on the concrete floor.

"Hi, Titán," I say cheerily. I speak his name with confidence and reach out to touch his mane. He acts as if I'm not even there and doesn't respond at all. Except that by ignoring me he is in fact responding! His message is clear but I choose to ignore it.

"Hi, Titán," I repeat, searching for an indication that he recognizes me. "I'm so glad to see you."

The horse looks up hesitantly, while chewing on a clump of straw. Then turns his focus to the saltlick in front of him.

"You are the one who first spoke to me, the first horse I ever heard speak," I say stroking his side. "It all started with you, Titán. Don't you remember me?"

He turns away, seemingly bored or perhaps just disinterested, and proceeds to nibble from the hay on the ground. But I still want his acknowledgement, and take his lack of recognition personally. Despite feeling rejected, I persist.

"Come on, now, Titán! I've come all the way over here just to say hello to you."

Titán lifts his head once again, grass sticking out of the sides of his mouth. For just a moment he stops chewing:

I suppose that I do recognize you.

He looks me squarely in the eyes.

It's just that we get so many visitors here and it's hard for me
to remember you all.

I am taken aback. My ego is bruised. How embarrassing.
What happened to my humility? I struggle with the horse's
reaction, but even more so with myself.

"See you later, Debbie," I say, taking my leave without both-
ering to greet any of the other horses. I spend the rest of the
morning in my cabin alone writing, thinking, and meditating.

"So what—as far as Titán is concerned," I figure. "It's
Beauty I am here to see. She's the one I need to connect with
on this trip." I attempt to console myself, and to justify my
behavior. But I know better; I was wrong. This gift isn't supposed to be about me. Aren't I supposed to "be the voice for
those who cannot speak?"

Just before lunch Debbie comes to see me.

"I've been thinking about you and Titán," she exclaims,
stretching her body out at the foot of the bed. I am heartened
by our friendship, and how good it is to have her in my life.

"Me and Titán? Oh; what about us?" I ask.

"What do you think was going on when Titán spoke with
you like that?" she returns, as if asking an innocent question.

"I guess he's a lot like me," I tell her. "He encounters different people here, every day. Of course he can't remember everyone he meets," I say. "So what? How is that significant?"

Judging by the determined look on Debbie's face I know
this will not be the end of our discussion.

"I don't know, Rosa. Maybe it was something else."

"Something else? Hum, like what?"

"I think Titán was giving back to you exactly the message you were sending to him. This is what horses do," Debbie continues. "They mirror what's inside of us."

Yes, but even if that is true, it doesn't entirely explain how Titán knew that I had forgotten what he looks like, or that I think I have too many people in my life to remember the individual horses in the herd. Debbie looks at me quizzically, her eyebrows raised. I recall the look in Titán's eyes as I stroked his mane in search of recognition. It was a touch of longing, I wanted my presence to be significant to him, and that my return visit would please him and be acknowledged. My ego needs had kicked in. How many other humans had he spoken with, or been understood so precisely as by me?

Admittedly, I wanted to be special, not seen as just another tourist. I wanted for him to remember me, uniquely. After all, Titán was the very first horse to speak with me. And it was Titán who was so surprised that I, as a human, could actually hear him. Have there been others since then?

"Let's go back and see him again," I suggest. "We'll find out if you are right about this."

I did not want to accept Debbie's premise, or admit to my shame. Debbie agrees and we ride her 4-wheeler back to the barn. Beauty, Conan, Gitana, and most of the other horses are in the barn when we return. I have come to care about this herd, and I want to believe they care about me. But their blasé reaction to my arrival is as if they do not know me at all.

We move along the center aisle. Debbie reminds me who is who as we make our way along the stalls. I greet each horse by name. I try to note any distinctive dapple, most of the horses being an indistinguishable brown. Some I do not recognize, simply because they were foals when I was last here. I sense something intentional in their nonchalance. I begin to suspect that they know exactly who I am, despite that they show no particular interest in me, their heads held down as they munch on hay, or lick salt from the feed containers. All the horses, that is, except for the mare Gitana. Her head is raised high. She stands very still, looking in my direction. She clearly wants to speak to me. I note how her belly is broadly distended. Debbie explains that Gitana is pregnant again.

"How are you feeling, Gitana?" I ask, moving to be by her side. Her reply is immediate. I can hear her clearly as she speaks:

I want this to be the last time. No more pregnancies after this one. I've been very tired with this one, but more than that, I am afraid. I saw what happened to Pica. I saw the blood and I watched her painful dying. Is that what's going to happen to me?

There had been a tragedy that summer. A mare named Pica had died giving birth to her foal. Early the next morning her body was found in the same field where the herd spends the night. Gitana continues her communication with me:

What if Debbie isn't here when I give birth? Who will care for me and help me if I need it? What happens if something goes wrong? I know that she is leaving soon. I don't want to do this without Debbie here with me.

The first time I ever met Gitana, and the first time she ever spoke with me, she was pregnant but her human caretakers did not know about it. Gitana was worried then too, aware that something was wrong, and she wanted to be left alone in the field for a while. After a few weeks she lost that pregnancy. Since then she's gone through another full-term pregnancy, without any problems. This time, however, she knows because she's witnessed just how wrong things can go during a delivery.

Debbie stands by my side, wide-eyed and somber as I translate Gitana's concerns. She seems anxious about this, her personal favorite horse.

"Rosa," Debbie asks me quietly. "Do you think that Gitana is just mirroring what I am feeling?"

Debbie explains that she's been anxious about leaving for her upcoming trip to the U.S., and especially about being away during the delivery of Gitana's foal. Even though Debbie didn't witness the event herself, the thought of Pica's death horrifies her. Debbie will be going away for an entire month. With Gitana's late-term pregnancy, Debbie is worried over what might happen while she is away.

I am not sure how to answer Debbie's question about Gitana mirroring her emotional state. I am still learning about horse-human relationships. I have read and been told that unlike humans horses live entirely "in the moment," without preoccupation about the future or the past. But Dorado proved that conviction wrong when he spoke to me about breaking my promise to the herd. It seems to me that at this moment both Gitana and Debbie are remembering the past, and using that to anticipate the future. Even if horses do reflect back to us what we are projecting, as Gitana may be doing with Debbie, horses certainly have their own feelings, fears, needs, and cares. And they are intelligent enough to associate an event of the past with a forthcoming, similar event such as the birth of a foal. In this case, even if she is responding to Debbie, Gitana is also worried about herself.

A few other friends and family members arrive at the retreat. That afternoon, Debbie takes us all on a trail ride to a waterfall. I had some hesitation about going on the trek because of the difficult terrain. What's worse is that in this, the rainy season, patches of the trail are deep gullies of mud. I join the ride despite my anxiety and mostly I manage okay. But on our return we take an alternate route, and have to cross a small river. The river is not the problem. My issue is that we have to go down a steep rocky slope in order to make the crossing.

I sit on Dorado's back looking down the hillside, at the boulders and rocks and mud, trying to navigate which will be the safest path to take. Meanwhile, nearly everyone else has passed us, and is already across. Dorado refuses to budge. I plead and kick him and yell, "get going," but nothing I do will make him move. Debbie rides up from behind me.

"What's the problem, Rosa?" she asks. I can tell that it's a rhetorical question, asked solely to make a point. But I answer it any way.

"I don't know what's wrong, Debbie. No matter what I do, this horse refuses to go," I complain.

"Maybe it's you who refuses to go," Debbie throws back. "Have you considered that he's only reflecting what you feel?"

"There's a thought," I say to myself, sarcastically. The fact of the matter is that I am terrified.

"Maybe you're telling him one thing with your body by kicking, but another thing with your mind," rolling her eyes in the way that only a good friend would do. Debbie is trying her best to teach me, and we'd been over this many times before.

"Which instruction do you expect him to follow?" she continues.

Her point is that Dorado is sensing my hesitation (the authentic feeling I am denying from myself), which is in conflict with my bodily movements and also with my words. Who did I think I was fooling? Obviously it was not the horse that was the problem here. It was my agitated inner state. I realize that if I am going to get back to the cabin on horseback, then my only option is to be honest with myself, and also with the horse. I acknowledge my fear and mistrust of Dorado. I regain my centered awareness with a slow exhalation. Immediately Dorado descends the slope, and we cross the river.

Only two more days remain before leaving for home. I am anxious to spend time with Beauty. But Beauty has yet to exhibit any interest in me. At a loss for how to break through to her, I begin to question my decision to come, asking myself, "Was her ethereal visit with me that morning last spring merely a fantasy?" Fretful and agitated, and thinking I have wasted both time and money; I take a long time to fall asleep that night.

In the dark of pre-dawn, a rooster crowing stirs me from deep sleep, though I soon fall back into dreaming. The sudden brilliance of sunrise startles me shortly thereafter, at 5:16 a.m. I note the lizard scuttling across the wall. Turning my gaze through the plate glass window, which frames an entire wall of the cabin, a hummingbird swoops across the porch. Out in the distance, the top third of the volcano is enshrouded in clouds. The sound of horses rustling in the field below, tells me the day has begun for them. But not for me; languishing on the bed, staring at the Arenal volcano, I doze off again.

When I reawaken at 7:30 a.m., this time it's for good. The clouds have dissipated to reveal Arenal in its totality; a perfect blue-grey cone from base to cratered top. This is an unusual and coveted sighting, especially during the rainy season. Sitting upright I place my feet on the concrete floor, and check my slippers for scorpions. (On a previous family trip to Costa Rica, my daughter Kaya saw a scorpion crawling across the floor near the bed in the hotel room. She was only six years old, and instinct rather than fear led her to pick up the nearest shoe and whack the predatory arachnid with a venomous stinger, hard enough to render it instantly dead.) Checking to be sure that nothing has crawled inside, I slide my slippers on. I shuffle into the bathroom and step into the open tiled shower. The cool morning air tingles my bare skin. When I turn on the hot shower, the moisture in the air sparkles under the sun's rays. Standing under the falling water, my mind wanders and wonders:

"What would happen if we were to gather a small group of the horses in the vínculo barn, and simply sit there with them, in silence?"

The vínculo barn is an open-air, metal-roofed structure used for training purposes and equine therapy sessions. Vínculo is the Spanish word for bond, link, or tie. Colloquially, in Costa Rica, the phrase "vínculo caballo" is used to refer to the sacred bond between horses and humans.

"What could we learn from the horses themselves, about the sacred bond they have with us?"

I dry myself off, pull on a pair of jeans and a tee shirt, and make my way up the road to the dining hall, excited about the idea. Horse trainer Shelley Rosenberg and psychiatrist Dr. Nancy Coyne, both equine-assisted therapy facilitators are already there, enjoying a "plato typico" (typical Costa Rican breakfast) of fresh fruit, fresh eggs, black beans mixed with rice, and fried plantains. I join them at their table. Debbie arrives towards the end of our meal. We discuss the therapeutic work the horses are doing with the teenage girls who are residents at a regional safe house. As childhood victims of sexual abuse, a few had been abducted, others forced into prostitution, some unsafe in their homes. The girls had come to the retreat for an equine therapy workshop, and as Shelly explained, the horses seemed particularly sensitive to the needs of each girl. Hearing this convinces me of the worthiness of my idea.

Nancy asks what I have in mind. I explain that the goal is to connect with the horses while we are in a meditative state of mindfulness. We will suspend all expectations of the horses and simply be open to whatever they chose to do, or to reveal. The women are intrigued. I continue to explain, surmising that once we are gathered there and sitting together in silence, the horses will be more open to communicating with us. It may take some time, I figure, and maybe nothing will actually happen. But my hunch is that at the very least we will learn something. They are willing to try it.

Shortly after our meal Debbie, Shelly, Nancy, and I meet down at the stable. As I sit on the cement center wall, silently telling the horses what we were planning, Shelly, who has a keen sense of horses, identifies those she intuits are responding to my message. Four in the herd indicate a positive response. I request that we add Beauty to the group, for a total of five. The horses are led from the stable into the vínculo barn.

We humans place four plastic chairs on the dirt-packed floor, in a U-shape at the far end of the barn. The five horses (Mr. Big, Amarillo, Stella, Titán, and Beauty) are untethered and freed to roam as they please. But before taking a seat I approach Beauty. She sees me coming and turns her head away. Nevertheless, I continue in her direction until I am close enough to touch her neck. Stroking her I speak in a whisper, "I came here because as you asked me to. Are you still wanting to speak with me?"

Beauty jerks away, pulling her ears back as a stern warning for me to get away. I retreat and sit down with the others, again questioning myself and my motives, even my decision to come here, thinking, "What have I done? Why is Beauty so angry with me?"

I close my eyes in prayer asking for help to remove any false expectations I may have of Beauty. I also use my inner voice to let the horses know that we are gathered simply to be with them and listen. It isn't more than a few minutes of sitting in silence before Debbie whispers,

"Look Rosa!"

I open my eyes to discover that Amarillo has moved himself directly in front of us. He stands very quietly and still. After a moment I hear him speak:

I just want to lie down. I give up.

I translate for the others, picking up that he no longer feels sure of his usefulness at the retreat.

Nancy suggests that perhaps Amarillo needs to "have his heart held." Volunteering to do so I rise and step forward, slipping one hand underneath onto his girth, and holding my other arm across his back. In this way I am able to intuit that Amarillo is feeling embattled with life, and is in search of some way to feel worthy. He stands still with me holding him, and then after a few minutes he walks away.

As soon as I sit back down Mr. Big approaches our group, announcing:

I am not frightened or sad the way I used to be. I feel safe here, secure and strong. My heart is not sick like before.

Mr. Big stands quietly in front of the four of us. I close my eyes to feel into him more deeply, and listen for anything further he may have to say. After a few moments I feel a shift: curious about this change, I open my eyes to find that Stella has pushed her way past Mr. Big, and is standing right in front of him! She moves to directly over my head, her eyes are staring down at me. Her declaration is quite clear:

No babies for me.

I translate as she continues:

I don't understand what happened to Pica.

Debbie speaks up, trying to explain to Stella what had happened to the pregnant mare, what it means when a horse dies, and about the finality of death. Stella seems to understand and lets me know what she wants Debbie to know; that she is highly intelligent but that she hasn't much of a motherly instinct. What she wants to do is to run. She says that one day she will surprise Debbie with her extraordinary racing capabilities.

Titán walks up, not in front but behind our chairs, looking back and forth between Debbie and Shelly. He leans in over my shoulder and asks:

What else do you need to know about me?

As far as Titán is concerned, everything is fine.

The horses act as if they actually understand our purpose; that we are there to watch, listen to, and understand what they have to say. None of us four women had ever experienced anything quite like this. We are flummoxed but also amazed that the horses seem compelled to respond to our being with them in silence. Other than Beauty, that is, who stays at the far side of the barn, looking everywhere except at us.

We return the five horses to the stable; I say goodbye and begin the trek back over the gravel road to the cabins. Nancy and Shelly are walking together, behind me by about twenty feet. When I begin to pass the corral Nancy calls out to me,

"Look, Rosa!" I stop and turn my head to see what she is talking about. Nancy is pointing towards Beauty who was standing on the narrow path that runs along the corral fence, which leads from the stable to the pasture where the herd sleeps at night.

"I think she is reacting to you," Nancy exclaims, explaining that just as I walked by, Beauty released a long exhalation. I shrug and continue to walk. I'd given up on Beauty.

A moment later I hear Nancy say, "That's two!"

Apparently Beauty has released another long exhalation. This time I stop, turning my gaze to her.

"Okay, that's three times now she has done that!" Nancy announces, excitedly. "She was staring right at you and audibly exhaling," Nancy persists.

"What does it mean?" I ask her.

"It's a sign of release," Nancy explains. "An expression of submission to you."

I am not sure why Nancy would think that the horse was reacting to me, because as far as I am concerned, Beauty has yet to even acknowledge my presence. Conceding Nancy's insight based on her training and experience with horses, she's given me something to think about. But our session in the vínculo barn has left me tired, and at this point I just want to rest.

VIII

Feel Into Your Inner Power

THE ECO-RETREAT IS OFFICIALLY closed to the public, with
an exception for a returning tourist family, there for the weekend. On the third day of my visit, after breakfast I am invited to
observe the family's boy and girl play horse games with Debbie
in the vínculo barn. Debbie is doing an exercise to teach the children to find and use what she refers to as their "personal power."

I take a seat behind the fence and observe from a distance.
The children seem excited to be there with the horse, and
without their parents. Debbie gives a brief explanation of how
horses, being prey animals, see humans as potential predators.
Then she explains the psychology of prey animals, how many
millions of years of adaptation and evolution have brought
the horse to a heightened state of awareness. Survival as herd
animals of prey depends on that awareness, since their lives
can be threatened at any time by predators that hunt and kill
them. She explains that as prey, horses need to know that they
are protected, and that those humans who care for them must
demonstrate the capacity to stand up to possible threats. So the
horses play the same games with humans that they play with
members of their herd, to clearly establish who has the power,

and who does not. The brother and sister grow fidgety with desire as they watch Debbie walk over to the fence and return with two whips.

Debbie explains how the children are to use their will to get the horse moving backwards and forwards. The Yoda character from *Star Wars* painted on the barn wall provides a familiar and motivating model. "Do like Yoda does," Debbie tells them. "Use 'The Force' to make your horse move." She demonstrates by flicking her hands and making a hissing sound, in order to get the horse to move backwards, as she wants him to go. The young boy and girl each practice for a while on two designated horses. The horses follow suit, willing subjects in the learning process. As for the children, they are clearly enjoying the feeling of such power, as to be able to move a very large animal without even touching him.

After they mastered the moving fingers and hissing technique, Debbie hands each child a whip. She tells them not to use it to hit the horse, only to use it to motivate him to move. Nancy and Shelly join me in watching as the girl of maybe seven and boy of about nine years discover and play into their sense of personal power. How satisfying and amazing each of them must feel to get such a large animal to move at their will. But I wonder, what, is actually happening? These children, whips in hand, did indeed seem to be directing the movements of the horses. Are the horses threatened by their gestures? These animals are much bigger than they, and towered over the children. The kids themselves couldn't be that much of a threat so I wanted to know, what was actually causing the horses to move?

At lunchtime I observed the same boy entangled in a match of wills with their mother. The two were in the restroom, arguing. The door was wide open and I was just outside, waiting my turn to use the facilities before eating lunch. The mother was insisting that the boy wash his hands, and the boy was resisting vehemently, claiming to have already done so. The mother won that battle, standing over the boy as he reluctantly placed his hands under the faucet. The boy was in tears. I recalled the same child's display of grandeur in the arena, as he coaxed the horse to back up on his command. I considered the force of his will against the horses', and what it means for one species to control another. But while moving the horse back and forth at will became a delightful game for the child, the maternal encounter was not a game. Or at least it was no fun for the boy being the one who had to relinquish control.

The mother and sister left the bathroom and went into the dining hall, leaving the boy sitting on a boulder outside, sobbing quietly. I felt for the boy, but also wished he could put himself in the place of the horse. The boy's frustration with his mother is understandable. What about when a horse is under the control of a human's will? Is it as frustrating and humiliating to the horse, as it was to the boy whose mother insisted on his following her will? Most people might think this an absurd question, seeing horses as lesser beings, animals that have been domesticated and trained entirely for human purposes.

I've observed horses entangled in a match of wills with another horse, in order to establish and maintain dominance hierarchy in the herd. That's a horse being a horse inside the domain of the horse herd. But how does a horse feel when challenged by a human being, who is claiming the power of control? Debbie reassures me that horses are relieved and comforted with demonstrations of power and control, and that my qualms are a projection of human ways onto the horses. For a horse, as animals of prey, demonstration of dominance provides assurance that in the presence of the dominating person, the horse and its herd are safe from the threats of a potential predator.

When I enter the dining hall Debbie, Shelly, and Nancy are enjoying a meal of freshly made chicken and bean empanadas. I share my frustration with the group. Beauty has still yet to acknowledge me directly, I tell them. And whenever I have approached her, she's shunned or threatened me with an aggressive stance, jerking her head away from my touch and baring her teeth when I have come too close. Confused about the mixed signals she's given me, I'd begun to suspect her behavior to be purposefully goading.

"Is it a matter of my will as opposed to Beauty's and establishing who is in control?" I asked the three experienced horsewomen. Shelly must surely know, as one who has been riding for over thirty years, is a United States Dressage Federation (USDF) "L" graduate, and a seasoned instructor. I told them I was back in Costa Rica because Beauty had come to me in a waking dream, and asked me to return. Shelly shakes her head with, "I don't know, Rosa."

Debbie, who is sitting right next to me, suggests that I play the "energy game" with Beauty. I sensed that Debbie was scheming, but couldn't fathom why.

"But with Beauty it's really hard," Shelley pipes in from the other side of the table. She is clearly intrigued. "If you do succeed with her you'll change, you know. It will completely change your world. Your relationship with Beauty and other horses will never be the same."

"It's true," Debbie echoes. "Beauty is a really tough one."

Beauty is the lead mare of the herd. She needs to maintain her position of power in the herd. Why would she submit to anyone, and especially to me? I am uncertain that I want to engage any of the horses in this way, and especially not her. The question on my mind is, "Haven't animals been dominated long enough?" I really don't see the point, and I am not particularly settled with the idea of it. But since Debbie, Shelly, and Nancy all agreed that it's exactly what I ought to do, I decide to try and see what happens. What did I have to lose?

Shortly after lunch the four of us meet back in the barn. Debbie has arranged for three horses, J.R., Mr. Big, and Beauty to be there when we arrive. Shelly uses J.R. to demonstrate to me how the game works. With a whip in her hand and a commanding voice she has J.R. trotting in circles. Shelly's demeanor is masterful and her confidence is strong. She is in total control of J.R.'s movements. When Shelly is ready to end the game, and not a moment before, she exhales and bends her body over in a bow, to let J.R. know that he now has her permission to stop. Once he does, as part of the protocol Shelly moves up to the horse and presses her hands down on his neck, until J.R. complies, lowering his head in submission. Once his head is bowed down to the ground, and he's acknowledging Shelly's power; the game is over. I am amazed, though uncomfortable with the entire exhibition; and yet there's something amazing going on here that I want to learn.

Debbie comes down off the rail and walks into the arena, announcing that she wants to show me something else. She goes for Mr. Big, the same horse who had explained to us that he no longer sees himself as broken and abused, now wholly healed and happy with his life. Stretching an arm out to her side, Debbie points a finger to indicate which way she wants the horse to go. With her other hand she cracks a whip on the ground right behind Mr. Big and in response, he runs part way around the circle. But instead of continuing, he stops right next to Beauty, who is standing in the corner of the barn, her attention seemingly focused outside of the activities in the arena. Debbie persists in working her command and strengthening her force of will, until eventually she gets Mr. Big moving again. It takes quite an effort on her part, and every time Mr. Big begins to respond, he trots around the ring only to stubbornly stop halfway, to stand besides Beauty. This goes on for a while until Debbie throws up her hands in frustration.

"What is going on here?" she cries out.

Shelley hops off the stool she had been perched on, and approaches the side rail. Leaning her arms over the top board of the fence, she calls to Debbie.

"Mr. Big is challenging you," she exclaims.

"What do you mean?" Debbie replies.

"He is letting you know that he is in his power, and that you are not recognizing him as well enough to handle yours."

Debbie lets out a sigh, and Shelly continues her coaching.

"It's obvious that you are holding back, tentative about what you want him to do."

"How so?" Debbie asks. Her elbows are extended, palms on her waist. She glances at Shelly, and then back towards Mr. Big, who is ignoring Debbie and looking towards Beauty.

"Mr. Big is not responding to you as you wish him to, because you have not yet insisted," Shelly reveals.

Shelly's words resonate as true to me. Ever since Mr. Big has come to live with Debbie at the cabin retreat, she has treated him gingerly and with great care, not wanting to exacerbate his emotionally compromised condition. Mr. Big had been brutalized in his prior occupancy. If she had cracked a whip at him when Mr. Big first arrived at Leaves and Lizards, it would have sent the distressed horse cowering into the corner. But Mr. Big had told us that he is fine now, that he is a healthy, happy, well-adjusted horse and wants to be seen that way. No longer the emotionally traumatized being he was, Mr. Big is filled with gratitude and appreciation

"You will lose this game every time you play it with Mr. Big," Shelly continued, addressing Debbie. "He won't respond to your commands until you change your assumptions about him, and stand strong in your power. This is what he is waiting for you to do."

I am moved by Shelly's interpretation of Mr. Big's behavior. It's compelling, what she says. These horses are especially sensitive and aware, attuned to the emotional state of the individual human beings that they encounter. What Shelly has suggested also makes sense since Mr. Big is grateful for all that Debbie has done to provide a safe and secure home for him. His motivations are out of loyalty and devotion. In his own way, in resisting her, Mr. Big is helping Debbie to become more self-aware, and more mindful in understanding the herd. Knowing relatively little about horses, I appreciate the opportunity to learn from Shelly and Debbie. Even so, I have to trust my own intuition, and my psychic sensitivities regarding what may be going on here.

I have a hunch that there might be another factor at play. Mr. Big's behavior, it seems to me, also has something to do with Beauty's being in the barn. Indeed, Debbie may need to alter her thinking about that horse, and to strengthen the display of her power. But my sense is that she is also working at cross-purposes to Beauty, who is pulling Mr. Big into her own energy field. Beauty wields a lot of power in the herd, on par with the stallion Jauno. I believe that Mr. Big is under *Beauty's*, rather than Debbie's command.

Debbie lays down the whip, walking across the dusty dirt floor of the arena to join us, the three observers seated at the side. "Your turn," she exclaims, looking at me as she approaches the group. "With Beauty, I mean."

I stand and Shelly stands too. Shelly instructs me to first center into my breathing, and then to scan my entire body, to establish my center of focus.

"Feel into your inner power," she coaches me, "and then use it to intrigue Beauty to follow you," she says. The purpose is for me to engage Beauty in a game of domination and submission, she explains.

"Really?" I wonder to myself. "How am I to prove to Beauty, a thousand-pound animal that towers over my head, and the lead mare to boot, that she should let me dominate her?"

I move into the arena, looking at Beauty, who is standing on the far side of the barn staring out across the gravel road, in the opposite direction. I hear Shelly's voice calling from behind me.

"Most likely," she warns, "Beauty won't respond to you at all, Rosa."

I pick up the whip that is lying on the ground. I am to use it to make Beauty trot—not by actually whipping her, but by intimating that I can and will do so if need be. I look at the whip, wrapped inside my palm, my fingers clasped around its leather handle. Something doesn't feel right, and I hesitate. "Were my great-great grandparents whipped as enslaved humans?" I don't want to force any animal (or another human for that matter) to submit to my will, solely to establish my power. I'd train a dog not to urinate in the house, and a cat to use a litter box to poop. I'd punish a dog for biting a child, and forbid a cat to claw at my wool carpets. But to wield my power just for the sake of doing so seems awfully master-slave-like to me. Why am I doing this?

Shelly, Debbie, and Nancy watch quietly. I am solemn, silent, standing still, in the center of the arena. Staring at Beauty and considering what to do, I remind myself of Debbie saying, "It's just a game to them!" I close my eyes and focus on my breathing, as Shelly has instructed. But what I do next is a deviation from the directions she's given me, on how to play the game: I put the whip down on the ground. Then I walk over to Beauty's side and whisper at her ear saying, "I have observed and honored your power. Now it's time for you to feel and respond to mine!"

"What is Rosa doing?" I hear Shelly asking the others, from their seats behind the rails.

"It looks like she's saying something to Beauty," I think Nancy replies.

"She won't be able to just talk her into this," Shelly returns. Their voices fade from my attention as I sense into Beauty's presence, her black eyes locking into a gaze with my own. She's no longer ignoring me. I feel her energetic response as a direct challenge, as if saying, "let me see you make me."

I step back into the center of the arena, picking the whip up, and taking a deep, grounding inhalation. As I do so, I imagine myself as being filled with a powerful, radiant blue energy. Beauty is still standing by the fence, to my left, only now she is looking in my direction. Exhaling, I extend my arm out to my left side, my index finger pointing. In my right hand is the whip. Taking in a deep breath, I snap it into the air and then smack it down onto the ground, yelling, "Huh!" The gorgeous black mare, with the white streaked face, takes off in a slow trot around the circle, her mane bouncing and hoofs lifting in a rhythmic gaiety. Debbie hops up from her seat, grabs a chair and a pole, and enters the arena.

"Here, make her jump over this!" she tells me as she balances the pole between the rail and the chair, creating a make-shift jump of about two feet high.

Once again I command Beauty to run, which she does for a bit but then she stops at the fence by the geldings, stubbornly refusing to move. As with Beauty, I have been exerting myself, turning and running behind her as she runs the circle, in order to keep the pressure on her. Out of breath, I pause to collect myself. Once my heart rate slows down a bit, I approach her again.

"We are not finished playing yet," I state. "You will continue to run," out loud in a voice that feels commanding and clear.

Using my creative mental capacity, I envision a burst of energy coming from me, and pushing against her rump. Then I whack the whip down hard on the ground, and forcefully holler another "HUH!" Beauty takes off running faster this time around. With me in the center using the whip, she jumps over the pole, before trotting back to where the other horses are gathered. Panting, she stands staring at me as if to ask:

"What are you going to do now?"

I catch my breath and close my eyes, centering in again, moving my awareness back down into my core. This has become a fun game, for both of us, it seems. There is a powerful, beautiful energy pulsating inside of me that I am now sensing. I realize that Beauty has sensed it, too.

"I think she is challenging you," Debbie yells. "She wants you to make her jump higher!"

I open my eyes wondering who is actually challenging me now: Debbie, Beauty, or both of them? I walk over to the makeshift jump, and lift the bar to the top of the chair, which raises it to about three and a half feet. The energy I now sense inside of me rises from my gut up into my chest, filling my torso with radiant power. Moving back towards Beauty I lock eyes with her, lift my left hand, and point for her to run to the jump. SMACK! I slam the whip down behind her rear hoofs. Beauty takes off running again, circling the arena, but she side-steps, trying to avoid the jump. Whirling behind her and yelling "HUH, HUH, HUH!" I throw more of my focused energy towards her, moving her back in the direction of the raised pole. Beauty jumps it, runs around the ring again, and then jumps it for a second time.

The women on the rail are whooping, and I feel great!

I had discovered the presence of energy and power inside of me. Able to stand my ground, I understood that such power is not about an egoistic need to feel superior, but about know-ing what and who I am in the core of my being. True power is about mutual trust, held and exchanged between one living being and another. I stand still. Beauty does as well. We face one another. I bend at the waist and lower my head in a bow, exhaling. We were done. Walking to Beauty's side, I place my hand on the top of her neck. Slowly but surely she lowers her head toward the ground, in honoring me. As she does I humbly honor her, beginning to realize why I have come here, and that Beauty's teaching had begun.

That night, lying quietly on my bed in the dim light of Coco cabin, I listen to the creatures that become active at night. The large plate glass window is black against the night, concealing the plethora of life on its other side. Creatures are drawn to the one incandescent bulb at my bedside, clamoring against the screens and glass in erratic flutters and bangs. They are persis-tent, desperate, it seems, to get to the source of the light.

IX

You Need to Forgive Your Mothers

THE DAY BEFORE I am scheduled to return to Virginia I wake up relieved and excited that I have finally connected with Beauty, yet also aware that my opportunity for contact with her will soon end. What had she meant by saying, "There's more for you to write about," during her ethereal visit with me back in the spring? Had I already gotten what I needed in order to begin writing another book? Or was there still more to learn from being with her? Assuming that she would be willing to participate I requested a meditation session in the vínculo barn, with just Beauty. Debbie agreed enthusiastically, though she suggested that we also include one of the geldings.

As before, Shelly, Nancy, Debbie, and I each take a plastic chair from behind the fenced arena in the observation section of the barn. We place them in a semi-circle on the dirt ring. The two horses roam as they please while we women shift into silence. But none of us is exactly meditative, quiet in anticipation, uncertain about what to expect yet hoping for something to happen.

Soon the gelding approaches, which he seems to do on Beauty's prompting. He stands nearby us for a while, as if curious but not communicating in any way I can perceive. Then

Beauty comes up and nips the gelding on the butt, sending him away. Once he is gone she moves forward, placing herself in front of us, in the middle of the semi-circle. As a result two of us are now positioned at the left side of her head, and two at the right. Her focus is beyond the arena, straight ahead. Silently, I thank Beauty. I also acknowledge the presence of the life force that makes it possible for me to be with her in this way. I am here to listen and to learn. I express my desire to be of service to the highest good of all concerned, and to be respectful of this gift. Using mindful-awareness of the breath, I shift consciousness into my heart, putting aside the egoic mental part of me that tends to assert control. I want to clear such interference, including the intellectual processes of evaluation and judgment. Past experience has taught me that being centered in a pure and open heart is the only way to hear what Beauty has to say.

From that meditative state I sense that something unfamiliar has begun to transpire between Beauty and me. It's like a part of me has fallen away, and in the empty space that remains, something arises as a kind of flowing. Whatever is flowing in me has a specific meaning that I am able to interpret. I open my eyes gazing at Beauty, and begin to translate what I am sensing her to be saying:

> I will speak to you about the energies available to us from the earth. There are primarily two, which you may most likely understand as feminine and masculine. Mostly what I see in you human beings is your struggles in attempting to access these energies. The feminine is the energy I know most about, as this is the one whose flow I have chosen to contain.
>
> There are two ways of carrying the earth's feminine energy. One is as a receiver, absorbing what others release.

This includes their fears, delights, desires, and pains, and sometimes the emotional basis of their illnesses. These flow from out of one human being in search of a willing receptacle to receive, contain, and in the best of situations, to transform into useful energy. It's the feminine that is most able to receive these energies of another. For those individuals who imbibe this aspect of the feminine, whose bodies and hearts are conducive, it requires putting aside the personal self in order to receive.

Beauty continues to stand very still directly in front of our group as I interpret the communicative flow between us. It takes me longer to speak the words than it takes for me to "hear" or receive the meaning being conveyed. She waits while I finish. And I then wait, unable to anticipate what may be coming next, until I feel the flow rising in me again.

The feminine is profoundly misconstrued among you humans. It has been taken for granted, disrespected, and misused. This is why there is so much physical and emotional abuse against humans who carry the feminine energy. They get seen as a dumping ground, rather than as the purveyor of the divine feminine. Why? Because of the many who fear being without access, desperate for the absorbing capacity. This makes them feel weak and vulnerable.

There is another pause in the flow. I turn my attention to the other women. Nancy the psychiatrist has been looking at Beauty, but is now looking at me, her hand placed under her chin as if analyzing what is happening. I wonder whether she is questioning my sanity or authenticity. Debbie, who started out leaning forward as if intrigued, is now leaning back. I wonder if she, too, is questioning me.

I try to keep myself from becoming dissuaded, or anxious in assuming my colleagues are judging me. I suspect that they think I am making this up, or am out of my mind. Indeed, this entire affair must seem strange to them, and would to anyone by conventional standards. But for me, personally, this encounter with Beauty feels entirely natural, and is giving me a wonderful feeling of satisfaction and joy. Despite our difference in species, something about her feels akin to what I am.

The second way feminine energy is carried is through providing support, nurture, and sustenance to another. In this case, the energy flows out rather than in, like rain that brings moisture to parched ground. It provides what others need to grow and thrive. The danger is when another pulls from the carrier, more energy than she has access to, in which case the carrier will become depleted. Working with either of these two forms of feminine energy can be draining if the carrier doesn't allow the energy to flow—if she mistakenly believes it is she that is its source, provider of the energy, herself. This can be treacherous for both provider and receiver.

For a moment I lose my confidence and begin to doubt myself. Is this "translating" a masquerade? Beauty turns her gaze in my direction. This restores my centered breathing, and reminds me to sense my heart. I vow to trust the process and have faith that we are in the Light. I tune back in and listen to the mare, continuing to translate what I feel into words:

Each one of you is in a compromised state, depleted at your core. You are exhausted and you believe it is because you work too hard, without getting enough time to rest. Think about this in another way and you will understand.

The flowing shifts when Beauty shares an image with me, which I see but not with my usual vision. The image is of a feed bucket similar to what is used for the horses; only it has a hole in its bottom. I explain to the others what I am seeing, and how Beauty is using that image to demonstrate why so many of us who carry the feminine energy are totally exhausted. She then continues:

You want to be giving and helpful to others, yet you are pouring your energy out into something that cannot contain it, into situations, places, and people that are out of alignment with the life force. You keep trying to win approval and recognition as a carrier of the feminine ener-gies. Despite your efforts this does not come. Instead, you are simply taken for granted. This is very risky for your health.

At this point it seems as if Beauty is talking specifically about me, which I explain after I have translated.

"What can I do about that?" I ask Beauty, out loud so that everyone can hear my question. The answer is immediate:

Find a situation where the people you are serving know how to receive what you have to give, a place where people appreciate and respect what you represent and who you are, glad for what you have to offer. Right now your own life force is running straight out of the bucket. No matter how much more you allow to flow in, it continues to flow right out. You are killing yourself.

Beauty lowers her head and her eyes close slightly, as if she is falling asleep. For a few minutes, there is nothing at all: No rising energy, no flow, just stillness, and I am not picking up any content from her. Respectfully, I hold the silence trying to remain open and present. Before long she begins again:

You need to forgive your mothers. Your pain and disappointments in them are interfering with your capacity to carry the feminine energy. Most women do not realize what they are doing. All they know is that they want to survive. This lack of forgiveness is eating away at the part of you that still seeks to protect that vulnerable child that you were. Forgiveness is your only way to get beyond it and to be whole.

Debbie's eyes widen and Shelly's do, too. Nancy begins to rub her chin. The words I am speaking, presumably an accurate representation of what Beauty is saying, are coming from somewhere different in me than the words I normally speak. But what, then, is their source?

Humans procreate in response to biological and social impulses, just like horses do. But humans do this without truly understanding what it means to mother another, of the energy that it takes. When the child requires more energy than a mother has access to, then she is literally drained of whatever is available. This leaves a woman feeling anxious and eventually resentful; once she senses the depletion of her own life force. Finally, in unconscious desperation, a mother will turn the flow around, pulling energy from the child's core in order to restore and sustain herself.

The women's faces grow somber. Tears well up in their eyes. Beauty's message is reaching us personally, and deeply. I feel emotions, but it's more like I am observing rather experiencing them. I attribute this distancing in me to the state of mind I need to hold to align with Beauty in this unusual mode of communication.

Beauty shows me another image. It's a mother holding her child, while extracting a flowing substance (which I take to be energy) from the child's chest. The mother draws it directly from the child into her own chest. This she is doing on the level of the energetic body, rather than as a physical process.

As I share this Shelly gasps. I look sympathetically at each of my friends; we all seem to be relating to this image.

I consider my own mothering. Have I have been able to support my children's well-being without literally sucking the life out of them? I recall the long nights with my nocturnal toddler who would not sleep and infant daughter who cried through the night from stomach pain. I did all I knew to do to tend to them both. At the same time I was trying to succeed at my job as a head of school and as a doctoral student. I was beyond exhausted as a young mother.

I also realize that I need to forgive my own mother. She once confessed, "I wasn't ready for you to be born." And to also forgive myself, for taking on way too much work responsibility while studying, mothering my young children, being in a marriage, and caring for our home. From where had I drawn my energy all those years?

I consider more recent times, and the ways my son and daughter toughed it out through the divorce. Can they forgive me?

My colleagues and I speak to one another, sharing thoughts and reactions, memories, confession of struggles with mothering, and being mothered. It dawns on me that we are in the presence of a wisdom being. I feel the flow begin again and place my finger to my lips in a gesture to alert the other women. The four of us grow quiet, listening as Beauty continues to speak:

When one's child or other loved ones fall sick, you seek to help by providing nurturing care. Thinking that you can do so from what strength you have inside, transferring some of your own energy to keep or make that child well, is a misunderstanding of how Earth's feminine energy works. You cannot do this without causing yourselves to suffer as a result.

The child's or other person's sickness belongs to them. You cannot remove it by replacing it with your own energy. Only when the feminine energy flows through you, and not from you, can you support another without causing harm. If you chose to carry the feminine energies, then you must continually resource yourselves by attracting and absorbing Earth's life force, allowing this to flow through you. Whereas the masculine energies are dispersed across the atmosphere in charged pulsations, they intertwine with the feminine, which come up directly from the earth. The masculine may be held and stored for use. The feminine must always be allowed to flow. Both can be transmitted by a human being, though there will be a preference, or a tendency toward one or the other.

In the human world, feminine energy has been corrupted. Most who want to have access don't know how to resource it for themselves. And yet your capacity to carry this energy is essential to the well being of the human world. The feminine energy is in huge demand because it is necessary to sustain life. This is one reason for so much of the chaos and sickness in the world. This result is a compromised condition not only for humans but also for all of life on the earth. Humans have disturbed the balance of the feminine and masculine for all the species. But all is not lost. It can be restored in yourselves, and on the earth, too.

"How does this show up in relationships?" one of us wants to know. Beauty answers:

Energy goes out willingly from the one who carries the feminine, in support of those who wish to receive it. But when it is hoarded by the carrier, and drained by the receiver, then the carrier becomes depleted, and resentment builds up, leaving relationships unstable. Sometimes when feeling depleted, the carrier of the feminine will reverse the process and withdraw energy from the very people she intends to support. The battle then begins over access to her energy. It manifests as discord in the relationship. Frustration, anger, hostility, and unhealthy environments are the result. Many families have created this exact dynamic. I see it every time a family comes to ride us. None of this is conscious. It is a desperate attempt to survive. You must forgive the mothers who do not understand how to take care of themselves, while also taking care of others. They are simply putting out more energy than they have accessed for themselves. All they need to do is to reconnect with the earth's life force to receive the feminine energy continually. Then they can allow it to flow.

Beauty adds,

"If horses did not do this, our herds would fall apart."

"Explain more about the healing," Debbie asks. As a former nurse, and in her efforts in Costa Rica to work with children who are ill, abused, or otherwise compromised, Debbie is first and foremost a healer. Beauty speaks to Debbie's personal mission in her work:

Children, who are victim to an energy struggle with their mothering caregivers, present as empty shells. For the horses, healing these children is easy, but is only a temporary measure. Once they are back in their home environments, the energy-sucking forces of their care-giving parents will empty them out again. It is fine for the horses here to help the children when they come, but their problems will return after they are gone. We are a superficial, temporary aid to them. For true healing, their mothers must first be healed. Your healing efforts should focus on the mother. Once she is well and able to re-source herself, then the family and children can also be well.

I wonder why human mothers have such difficulty maintaining and managing their energy needs, in caring for themselves and others. Is there a limit to how much we can hold inside? When I ask these questions out loud, Beauty responds.

It is always a choice whether and how to accept the feminine energy. FLOW is the key. Humans who have it tend to
think of this energy like gold you can own, as something to
be cherished, squandered, or protected for use in your own
purposes. When it is in your interest to share it, you dole
it out in small portions or large, depending on the situation and what it requires of you, and depending also on
what you think you may get in return. But the life force of
our Earth cannot be stored that way. You can step into its
flow and allow it to move through you, or risk depletion.
Horses don't even have to think about whether and how
to do this. It's a spontaneous process, something we learn
from our mothers and other mares, feel, observe, and imi-
tate. You humans attempt to hold onto the energy you are
able to absorb for fear of not having enough. Paradoxically,
this cannot be sustained.

Beauty has been standing before us nearly motionless for
almost an hour. This is highly unusual behavior for an untethered horse. She makes no indication of wanting to leave, or of
intending to go. Each time I interpret her message Beauty nods
her head ever so slightly as I speak, before continuing.

Shelly, Debbie, Nancy and I look at one another. We are
all clearly amazed. What is going on here? How can his be happening? These don't sound like the words of a horse. Obviously
I am using my own vocabulary to interpret the meaning of
Beauty's communication. There are times when I have listened
to horses and heard specific and literal words from them. But
this time it's different; I am sensing content without hearing
actual words, coming from somewhere deep in myself, but also
beyond the confines of my own mind. It is as if Beauty and I are

connected and communicating through something greater that encompasses us both. I feel myself to be in the same "flow" that Beauty is describing, accessing something intelligent, though what that is, I do not know.

Among the four of us, all is quiet for a few moments after Beauty has answered our questions. Then Shelly notices that Juano the resident stallion, who has been tied up to a tree just outside the arena, has extended his penis. We laugh, uncomfortably perhaps, not knowing why he is doing this. Almost as if in response to Juano, Beauty begins communicating again:

The presence of the masculine energy field is essential for feminine energy to be held strong. One very powerful source of the regenerating life force for the carrier of feminine energy is the masculine energy field. But when misunderstood and misused, the masculine energy can do great harm. It can be used to restore and recharge the feminine through the sexual act of penetration. Not simply physical penetration, but an energetic one, intended for this supporting purpose. But most human males who have chosen to carry the masculine energy have forgotten the purpose of the sexual act: besides providing the physical material for reproduction, they provide energetic support as well.

When the sexual act becomes entirely an act of self-pleasuring, rather than an act of giving, it further drains the feminine energy from she who holds it. There is a way in which the male can channel the life force through himself into her, but it is a rare human male that knows how to make that happen. The results are obvious. Rather than being restorative, sexual intercourse becomes depleting for the carrier of the feminine. Ideally, the feminine-masculine energetic exchange provides a source of life-force energy for both—for the male in the process of release, and for the female in the process of receiving. Such a dynamic exchange, which can also happen through other forms of energetic contact, invigorates the life force for us all. When held in balance in this way, there is enough life force flowing for every living being on Earth.

Beauty is an example of what she is describing, a being that holds and carries the feminine energy as receiver and sustainer. The geldings of the herd and the young ones too, seek her out in a competitive display, wanting to be near her. They compete for her attention. Is this because they are attracted by the feminine energy flowing through her? She maintains her health and her strength as she regulates that flow within the herd, receiving and releasing, restoring herself when needed, in order to provide for herself and her foal. Beauty is able to fulfill her role in the herd as lead mare because she knows how to keep replenishing herself.

Obviously addressing me, repeating what she had said before, Beauty says:

You are killing yourself.

"But how?" I want to know. I feel that what she is saying is an accurate description of my current state, but I don't understand what I am doing, or what I might do to change in order to be well. She looks at me and I feel something in her gaze, something that surpasses a single horse in wisdom and in intention.

. You have fallen out of rhythm with the pulsations of the life force. You crave access to the feminine energies, but are entrapped by the masculine. This state is making you sick and tired. And yet you know better. You know how to tap and maintain that force but have ignored the signs of depletion, adapting yourself to a human-made institution dominated by the masculine, which demands the release of your energy in sporadic, erratic, and highly-charged ways in order to assure your success.

But how does Beauty know this?

I close my eyes in reconnecting to the sense of flow. I wonder what I must do to receive and connect to the flow of feminine energy, sufficient to support and sustain me while I, in turn, support and sustain those I love. Beauty seems to be saying that the reason why so many human beings are desperate in their dependence on carriers of the feminine energy is because most of us do not know how to re-source it for ourselves. There is sufficient life force available on this planet to support and sustain us all. But many of us, apparently including me, have unknowingly cut ourselves off from Earth as its source. Perhaps this is a primary cause for much of the discord in the world.

I thought she had finished, but I was mistaken. My reflections are interrupted when I feel Beauty again. As she continues speaking I translate for the group:

What you have done to one another, in your desperate search for life-sustaining energy, you have also done to the earth. Knowing that the earth is a tremendous source of physical energy as well as the energy of life, you have reached into its core and extracted what you believe you need to support your way of life.

I consider the acquisition of resources like coal and crude oil that we extract from deep inside the ground and our more recent efforts to tap energy from the sun, the wind, and water. Beauty is referring to energies different than these, though they are not unrelated; energies that we cannot mine or hold or store for later use.

At some point the mother is no longer needed to sustain the life of the baby when the baby learns how to sustain itself. This is under the healthiest of circumstances. What has happened, instead, is that human mothers have forgotten this knowledge, and so they are not able to teach their children how to access that life force. The children then resist releasing themselves into the flow, turning either back to the mother for it, or seeking it elsewhere in other relationships, or in addictions. The herd here sees this in most of those who come here and ride on our backs.

The feminine and masculine energies of which Beauty speaks are accessible only through an individual's energetic field with intention and awareness. We cannot see these energies, or use machinery to collect and retrieve them. Which is why it's so easy to dismiss such a claim as nonsensical. In this way, the word "energy" may be easy to misconstrue. Nonetheless, these energies exist and if Beauty is correct, then they are essential to our wellness. Beauty says she sees the depth of depletion in the humans she spends time with. She suggests that the problem has to do with forgetting our true nature as connected to and sustained by the Earth. Is it that the life force that quickens us in utero, and leaves at our death, is somehow connected to the energies of Earth?

After the others leave, Debbie suggests that I work with Beauty to do a body scan. I am intrigued as Debbie explains, "Close your eyes and moving from head to toe, note where in your body a particular place becomes evident."

I follow her instruction; it's the tension and tightness in my throat, the clenching of my jaw, and a dull ache in my left arm that grab my attention.

"Which of these should I focus on?" I asked Debbie, my eyes still shut.

She suggests that I check again to determine which part of my body is speaking the loudest. This second time I do the scan I am most aware of a thick band of tightness across the back of my neck.

"Now open your eyes," Debbie instructs. "Look directly at Beauty. See if she has anything to say."

I decide to ask her directly what's going on in my neck. And Beauty says:

You are resistant to so many good things; some are presently with you, others moving in your direction. You are even resistant to closeness in relationships, and to those who love you and who you love.

I feel like I'm made of glass. How can she know this? This may be true but it is rather difficult to accept.

That resistance comes from your childhood, where for you own protection and the protection of your boundaries you learned to resist, even with your maternal relationship.

She speaks of my mother and me? This it is exactly what I need to hear.

It's no longer necessary to carry this pattern. It is causing you to resist the work that is coming to you and through you. It is detracting opportunities. Things are not coming to you that would otherwise be rushing in your direction. You need to make a shift.

That's enough of that. "Hey Debbie," I call out. "I'm finished with this scan exercise."

Debbie suggests that now I play the leadership game. She instructs me to go up to Beauty and get her to follow me. I try to do this, standing in front of her then walking away. Not only does she not follow, Beauty turns her backside to me, which I take to mean that she is rejecting my advances. (I have since then learned that this is a gesture horses will use to designate they are offering themselves. It was not the insult or rejection that I took it to be, but rather, a sharing of her most powerful self.)

"It's not working. What am I supposed to do?" I shout to Debbie, who is perched on the railing watching.

"Make her interested in you and she will follow you. Let her feel your leadership."

"What's that supposed to mean?" I think to myself. I've had leadership jobs before and I was pretty darn good at them. So this should be fairly simple. I'll just remember what it feels like when I am in a leadership role and then she'll want to follow me.

I try again with that attitude. But Beauty still doesn't move. Debbie explains that there's got to be something of me that she wants to be part of, something I feel inside myself. Debbie suggests that I smile in order to bring forward my inner joy.

So I smile, but I guess it must have been a fake one because once again, the horse remains just where she is. Is there something I am not doing, not feeling, or not realizing about myself?

I close my eyes and center into the core of my being until I sense radiance, a beautiful vibration inside of me! Feeling that I take a few steps, not even thinking about Beauty or what she is doing. I move in delight of what I am feeling. Beauty follows right behind, making every move I make to the left, then to the right, and even when I walk in circles. This was about sharing energy as opposed to leading from determination and will. But when for a moment I began to feel pride in getting her to follow me, she walks away. Moving back into that joyful state, when I walk she comes up behind me again, following wherever I go. For a moment I wonder, doubting my capacity to maintain her attraction to me, and I turn around to check on her. Beauty stops and looks away as if losing interest in me. She was completely aware of my state of mind in real time, attracted and compelled to follow not when I wished for control, but only when I was aware of and centered in my own inner beauty.

After we return Beauty to the stable, Debbie and I walk up the hill just beyond the barn to the tree where the stallion Juano is staked. (Juano has to be kept at a distance from the herd, or else there may be unwanted pregnancies, and fighting among the geldings! Since he likes to see the other horses, they sometimes keep him staked near the barn.) Juano is stunningly handsome with an auburn coat, golden mane and haunting, dark brown eyes. As explained in *When the Horses Whisper*, the first time I ever met Juano back in 2010 I felt an overwhelming attraction to him as being a very unusual horse.

Debbie puts a halter over his head and we begin to lead him down to the road, intending to take Juano back to his field. But Juana stops just as we reach the bottom of the hill and are about to turn onto the gravel road that leads to the field. He refuses to move any further.

"What's wrong, Juano?" Debbie asks him. "Don't you want to go back so you can graze?"

It was baffling behavior. Juano much prefers the freedom of the field to the confinement of being tied up. Debbie tries again to pull him in that direction. He resists with his thousand-pound body, decidedly not going anywhere.

"Rosa?" she turns to me. "Do you think that Juano wants to talk to you?"

Indeed, Juano had been watching the whole time that we were in the barn with Beauty. It made total sense to me that he would also want to be heard. On all of my other visits I have taken the time to speak with Juano. Here I was preparing to leave without having spent any time with him.

When we turn in the direction of the barn Juano comes along willingly. Steve, Debbie's husband, notices us going inside the barn with Juano, and comes to join us. We release Juano to roam freely, and sit quietly on the plastic chairs.

For fifteen minutes or so, Juano simply stands by the barn gate looking out toward the road. I close my eyes and speak to him in the silence of my mind, expressing my willingness and desire to listen to him.

"You are a great stallion," I say. "Forgive me for planning to leave here before you and I have had a chance to speak."

I genuinely meant what I said and Juano responds right away. He comes close, standing right before us and says:

Beauty told you about the feminine energy. There's more that you must know to have a correct understanding. You cannot write about the feminine energy without knowing about the masculine. Even though you think you understand the masculine since you seem to be entrenched in it, you have no way of knowing what this is actually like.

For those of us who chose to carry the masculine energies we first have to learn to manage what happens to our bodies. When I sense a mare in heat, my first and only concern is how I am going to mount her. This is not simply a thought. It becomes an all-consuming obsession until she is no longer in my range of awareness, which is not just about what I see. I am aware of her energetically even when she is out of my view.

As the only stallion in a herd surrounded by mares, my body tells me "there's one, there's another one, and there's another one that I must penetrate." This is the condition I am in, carrying the masculine energy. But it's only just one part of what it means.

And then he drops his penis, extends it, stiffens it, and swings it back and forth as if to say, "Now *this* is what I am talking about!"

"Rosa!" Steve exclaims, "What is Juano doing?"

I can't' help but chuckle. The stallion is providing me with a visual representation for the energy he is relaying. Juano continues to speak:

Many of the human males who visit here are like the geldings of the herd. They know they are males but they don't
feel it fully. They sense their capacity to function as those
holding and carrying masculine energy, but they don't
know how to do so. They function without confidence in
their capacity to sustain that energy inside of themselves,
because they were never taught how to do it. It's as if something essential is missing but they don't know what that is.
They are desperate yet don't know where to find it. As a
result, some become physically abusive to those who carry
the feminine energies (mostly females), and sometimes to
the young.

Juano stops the flow of communication to show me an
image of a male human being using a stick to hit a female. Then
he continues where he left off:

Others become emotionally or verbally abusive. Some are
kind and caring but don't know how to bring the masculine
forward fully enough to provide support to the feminine, so
they turn their attention away and focus on something or
someone other than the one holding the feminine energy.
They are participating in the world and in their families in a
compromised condition. They don't know how to stand in
display of their masculinity. It has nothing to do with domination and control. Masculine energy does have qualities
of strength, protection, and capacity for battle. But in its
essence, it is the capacity and desire to balance and support she who carries the feminine.

"How can he know this, Rosa?" Steve asks me. "This doesn't sound like a horse. What kind of being is he? An alien or something?" he tosses out, half-joking.

It was a reasonable query. We know horses to be our pets, our laborers, our entertainment, or our property in pursuit of earnings in showings, sales, and racing. We don't know them to be intelligent in the way the Juano seems to be; wise, aware, and observant of human beings. Juano waits as I reply to Steve.

"That's a good question," I say. "But unfortunately I don't have an answer. This is new to me, too. Until I came to your cabin retreat I'd never had the kind of encounters with an animal that we are having now."

Juano goes on:

Beauty needs me. Her work in the herd is very difficult because she has so many geldings present. The geldings are capable of holding the masculine, but not fully and completely, which means that her work is more complicated than it might be under the more natural horse herd living conditions. She needs my support. Even though I am usually physically separated from her, I am in communication with her and I am sending energy to her. The one who holds and channels the feminine energy absolutely needs the presence of one who holds and channels the masculine. The one cannot function without the other because the balance is essential. This has little to do with transmission of sexual material or with the act of mounting and sexual penetration. Though that behavior can play a significant role.

It's nearly dark now. Juano turns and stands over by the gate to indicate that he is finished speaking with me and ready to go back to his field. I walk with Debbie as she takes him down the dirt road to the entrance of the lower field. As his bridle is released I first ask his permission, and then touch his cheek as my way of saying, "thank you." Juano trots off into the night.

"I wonder if he gets lonely out there," Debbie says. I am thinking that he does.

My last night in Costa Rica is a strange one. There are so many questions to consider regarding the significance of what Beauty and Juano have said, particularly in terms of relationships between human men and women. Lying on the bed and despite attempting to go to sleep, I remain wide awake and thinking. I ask myself, "What is happening when I translate what I feel Beauty and Juano to be saying? Their words come out as if they were mine and it is me who is speaking, but the ideas are not familiar to me." I consider that perhaps I have taken this all too literally. Maybe the messages from the horses are best interpreted generally, regarding the importance of the connection between men and women, and the earth that sustains us all.

I lay quietly in the dark, my mind turning to what Beauty had said to me earlier in the day when Debbie and I were resting with our arms clasped and laying across Beauty's back:

With regard to you communicating with horses and writing about it, you are still waiting for the world to give you permission. External validations can be valuable and important, but you have to know more than anyone that who you are and that what you are doing is worthy. You don't believe that yet. You will have to believe it before opportunities will open for you to be able to further this work. A lot of time has already gone by in your life and it's time now to accept what and who you are.

I turn over to curl up, finally feeling I can fall asleep. But I sense that Beauty is close to me, wanting to be heard.

"I am listening," I whisper.

A response comes immediately:

In ancient times in the human world, feminine energy was pervasive and strong. Eventually, masculine energy supplanted the feminine and took complete control. Since then there has been confusion and conflict between males and females. We can see that the masculine energy is now beginning to weaken. But the situation is not healthy. The feminine energy is rising quickly, but it cannot be sustained without the active presence of the masculine. The imbalance is dangerous to those who are carrying the feminine. But the masculine energy is so corrupted, so compromised, and so misunderstood, that humanity's continued existence is uncertain.

Feminine energy, the creative life force, rises up from the Earth. It is provided by the Earth and is available still and plentiful where Earth has not been abused, but its access is lessening and more difficult due to abusive, destructive human practices and activities. Both males and females need this energy for survival. Those who choose to act as carriers of the feminine energy, serving in support of life itself, need to have consistent access to that flow.

Masculine energy, or the support for creation, falls to Earth from the sun and other celestial bodies that are in orbit around Earth. Though it is still plentiful and available, the purity and consistency of that energy flow has been disrupted by an array of human activity in the sky, on the surface, and beneath the earth.

All life forms draw from these energies. Humans, horses, and other animals also draw from both the masculine and the feminine. One of the features that distinguish human animals from others is the capacity to choose which energies to draw from and carry most directly, and in what way.

Human life, other animal life, and plant life in many forms are increasingly threatened with extinction. This is because the energy which sustains life, the feminine which rises up from Earth and the masculine which falls to Earth are no longer available with the consistency and balance that is needed. Humans know this; they can feel it and they are frightened, panicked by the disruption. But most are not fully conscious of their knowledge, only that they lack energy, feel anxious, or are depleted beyond what seems natural. They are seeking ways to replace what is more and more difficult to access directly. But their efforts are largely misdirected and their solutions are largely destructive. The result is imbalance, emotional and physical sickness, and a sense of emptiness in human life. We can feel this when you take your trail rides on us, when you come to play games with us, when you use us in healing others. We can see it when we observe you. We can sense in you what you are barely aware of in yourself. We have become aware. We see and sense what is happening to humans and to Earth. When you become fully aware you may be frightened. You may panic. The problem is quite serious.

We are here to help.

I sit up and write down what I have just heard. Then turning out the light, and settling back into repose under the sheets, I say out loud:

"Beauty, if this is real and we are really communicating like this, then I will need a sign, some kind of indication of what and who you are."

A few hours later I am awakened by a startling dream. In it I am looking up into the night sky through a large plate glass window that is straight over my head. Dense clusters of stars have formed against the blackness, suggestive of an astrological formation. I wonder which constellation it might be. Soon I realize that what I am seeing is the outline of horse's head, its mane and neck, face and eyes all formed by the stars. And this horse is looking directly at me! The white marking along the face, the dark mane hanging along her neck, the wide black eyes make Beauty's form unmistakable.

"Beauty, it's you!" I yell out, which is what wakes me up.

The clock on the nightstand indicates that it is 3:40 a.m. I sit up and look through the plate glass window of the cabin, toward the moonlit volcano straight ahead. I notice that above the volcano is a cloud formation that looks like a smooth dome, with a sharp-edged round bottom, formed over the top of the volcano. I sit in wakeful awareness, observing the cloud in its position, hanging so perfectly around the top of volcano. No longer feeling sleepy I close my eyes for inward meditation. After a while my body begins to quake, as if the earth itself is moving and shaking beneath me. Intuitively, I steady my breath to inhale and exhale calmly as my body continues to gyrate. After it subsides, I am left with a wonderful sense of vitality, as if recharged from a source greater and more powerful than myself. With my purpose now fulfilled, I am ready to return to Virginia.

Nancy, Shelly, and I happen to be traveling on the same airplane back to the United States. As we wait near our departure gate at the San Jose airport, Nancy shares an insight she has about me. Not only is she a fine horsewoman, she is also a psychiatrist with many years of clinical experience. I take her comments seriously.

"I've watched you with horses other times before," she begins. "I have observed as you have translated into words their hurts, their desires, and their concerns. I've been amazed at how accurate you are about their medical and emotional ills. But this time it was different. With Beauty I mean. What you were doing is not what you have done before."

Indeed, it felt different to me, too. I brace myself for an accusation or a challenge to my authenticity. I try to not to become defensive with Nancy, someone I respect so deeply. As Nancy continues I listen with openness:

"What I think is happening is that Beauty is acting as your muse. She is making you aware of something inside of you. She is helping you to bring it forward."

My muse?

X

Waking to Beauty

SEVEN MONTHS HAD PASSED since my last visit to Costa Rica. I'd put the writing aside to focus on my personal life and professional obligations. Bill and I were married in the spring, and then moved homes twice after that. There was also the matter of completing an academic book I was under contract to write. And my son Ari was on my mind, so I spent time with him. Those were among the reasons I had put *Waking to Beauty* on hold, but the truth of the matter was that I was losing my sense of purpose and my confidence in the work. What was I trying to accomplish in writing about my life and what I was learning from the horses? Was this really something I was meant to do? I'd already risked my status as a serious academic scholar by writing *When the Horses Whisper*. With this sequel, what would become of my professional standing? I hesitated, put the project away for a while, and then resumed in the spring.

One Sunday afternoon in April, Bill and I were on retreat in our mountain cabin. I was writing when an emotional upwelling overtook me.

"I have to go back to Costa Rica," I said to Bill, who looked up from his reading to find tears in my eyes. "I have to go back, soon."

Ten days later I arrived at Leaves and Lizards during an Epona training program.

"Don't mind me, I'm here to write," I told Debbie.

Debbie was respectful of my purpose and gave me the space and privacy I needed to write. It would be a short visit, and in wanting to support my project she also offered to bring to me any of the horses with whom I wished to communicate. I wasn't entirely sure why I was there, though I was glad I had come. I focused on writing, and on occasion went to the stable to greet the herd.

"Would you like to spend some time with Cosmo, Beauty, and Juano?" Debbie offered one afternoon. "I have a break for a few hours and the three of them would be available."

Debbie and I met shortly thereafter in the Vínculo barn. Three of the women taking the workshop also came to observe. Cosmo was already there, and after I took a seat and settled in he moved in my direction.

"Is there something you'd like to say?" I ask him. "I am willing to listen."

Being human you can't yet grasp the enormity of the abilities of animals and so I prefer not to talk.

I wasn't going to waste my time if that is what he felt. And I tell him so. After a few minutes he says,

I do like you, but you are still a human.

"A human who is willing to listen to other animals," I reply.

He walks away and I remain still, bringing the focus of my attention to my heartbeat and breath. I continue to speak to him, though silently, letting Cosmo know that I am listening and willing to share anything that he might want for me to communicate to the others. I hear it when he begins speaking again, even from the physical distance now between us. He scolds me for overlooking him for the more "attractive" horses during my previous visits. He tells me that he has no interest in fluffing my ego by speaking to me. He says that humans are very new to the earth and although we seem to think we are the highest form of intelligence, we are actually far from it. I translate all of this for the others and Cosmo continues:

> You humans look at animals and categorize them by what they can do for you. You breed this one with that one to improve on what you think is best, for your needs. When you look at animals it is only for how they can serve you. Horses are ancient beings capable of more than you can imagine.

I'd met Cosmo previously, while participating in various workshops at Leaves and Lizards. I'd had brief encounters with him, but this was the first time he has spoken to me this way. He is correct that on previous visits I'd passed him over. I'd found him to be uninteresting and saw him simply as a common horse to be used for riding. I am amazed that he picked that up about me and had remembered.

Cosmo has said what he needed to say. But he is also pleased with me. This I know because he walks back over and with his mouth on my shoulder gently nudges me. Then he walks to the gate indicating he wants to leave.

"Thank you, Cosmo!" I call out as he goes.

Debbie has Juano the stallion brought in next. Juano keeps his distance from the group but I can hear him. He speaks about how human beings have forgotten how to connect themselves to the earth to receive the energetic flow that fortifies the lower energy fields of the body.

"Well, how do we do that?" I ask him. He responds with specific instructions:

Place your feet on the ground, and draw it up from the earth and into your bodies, like the lungs do when breathing air. In a slowly moving flow, this grounding powerful energy will move into, and around the pelvis, then back out of your bodies down into the ground. This is the source of rejuvenating strength, which helps you to hold your entire energy field in alignment with Earth and with each other.

I try to do what he has suggested, uncertain that I can actually feel anything. I trust and believe that his teaching is valuable. Perhaps it will take practice. Juano continues:

Human males no longer feel the power of this connection, which leaves them without the capacity to share in a flow of their own energetic field of power, with human females. And as a result, human females have to do this for one another, in addition to doing this for themselves.

I am aware of how healers have advocated bringing the masculine and feminine energies into balance within the individual person. But this is different from what Beauty has said, and what Juano is saying now; that it's the balanced flowing of these energies between and among individuals (not just in the individual), which sustains the wellness of people, the family, and of communities.

"Human females shouldn't have to feel so vulnerable," Juano said at the end of our session.

When I was here the previous October, on the morning of my departure, Beauty and her son Rio were together in the stable when I went there to say goodbye. As I observed her with him I could see the care she was giving as more than just physical or emotional. As I sat on the concrete ledge that divides the two sides of the stable, Beauty leaned her neck into my leg and I gently stroked her head. She spoke to me saying,

> He is with me now because he is young, and I am supporting him with the feminine energies. But soon his father will teach him about the masculine, and how to use those in support of the herd. Right now, Juano is watching from a distance, supporting me as I support this young horse.

That young horse, whose name is Rio, is son to Beauty as sired by Juano. He looks exactly like his father, with an auburn coat and golden mane. But Rio is a gelding now, and will never be the stallion his father is. He has grown to nearly full height in the eight months since I saw him last. And I wonder over his capacity to use and move the masculine energies.

Beauty enters the barn after Juano leaves. As a follow-up to that last time, Beauty had spoken to me with Rio by her side, I asked her what happens to the transmission process of masculine energies to the son, when a male father is separated by physical distance.

It is possible through intention to send masculine energies to the son, even if physically apart. But what's not possible in separation is for the newborn baby to receive those energies from its mother. The newborn needs to be in the mother's aura, where she can support the baby while the baby is learning to bring those energies into itself. In the co-mingling of their auric energy fields, the baby learns from the mother how to bring those energies into its own body, so that when the weaning is complete, and the foal is functioning independently, it can do this for itself. The suckling process is also involved. It's not just delivering nutrients of the milk to the baby, but the baby is also receiving some supportive subtle energies. This is true for all mammals, including human beings.

I ask what are some of the reasons why humans are so exhausted, particularly the females, and she said it is partly due to the way we live; partly by the way our communities have been fractured; and also by the nature of our relationships with one another. So in the lifestyle part, she was talking about the necessity of having bare hands and feet making contact with Earth periodically, and that most of us just don't do that at all, and so we don't have that direct source of Earth energy. I considered that modern children don't play as much as they once did outside and in the dirt, which means they are not getting all the energetic support they need for their development.

Beauty has more to say about human females.

A lot of the females are untrusting and so they are closed off to receiving the transmissions of masculine energy from human males. This is because of the nature of the relationships and also because some of the males have forgotten that part of their responsibility, and what they end up doing is taking vital energy from the female, rather than exchanging energies with the female. Most humans don't know what is supposed to happen. In addition to the procreative aspect of the genetic material going into the womb, there is also an energetic flow from the male, which brings support to the womb. It also brings protection to the womb and to the female. The male has an interest in protecting the pregnancy, and also the female, more generally. Because of the draws that are made on her energy during pregnancy, she needs to be supported and restored through that exchange. Most human males don't know about that part of sex, partly because they are afraid due to their own neediness. They don't understand who they are or what they are meant to do, they don't know about their power and how to get to it. For these reasons they usually end up taking more energy than they give. And in taking more than they give, it depletes the woman.

What is supposed to happen is a co-mingling of the masculine and feminine energies, where the male receives from the female and the opportunity to release actually feeds him, and in the process of releasing he is providing an energetic support, not just semen. Part of the reason you are so exhausted is that it is not happening that way for a lot of you, and it's just a depleting process for males and females. In the case of animals that only copulate for reproduction, it's much less of an issue because the intention is clear. In the case of animals that copulate for pleasure as well, the intention is clear because this is what they know. In your case, the intention is not clear because you have so many other interests in mind; pleasure becomes a distraction. It doesn't have to be sacrificed, it can be part of it, but it can be a distraction. Over time it has made you forget the fuller energetic aspects of the sexual act.

"What is she saying now, Rosa?" Debbie asks, noting the way my facial expression has changed.

"She is switching to what happened in ancient times," I reply. "Talking about how women use to have direct access to those forces."

As women you can bring the feminine energies directly up into your bodies. But once it was discovered by powerful men that you have direct access to Earth's life force energies, women started to be manipulated like animals are now; owned, traded, and punished for not giving over what they had access to. This is really, really old - an ancient problem.

One of the motivations behind owning the female and rights to the female was the right to the offspring and what they represented. But a very big part of it was about the feminine energy. There were those who insisted on having direct access to that.

It seems clear to me, based on what Beauty is saying, that male and female human beings need each other. Or, that at least there needs to be a balancing of masculine and feminine energies in our relationships. But Beauty is also talking about how that need, once it loses the heart connection and becomes focused just on the lower aspects, leads to depletion and struggle.

> The result of your changes in sexual activity, from an exchange of energies to the domination of the feminine, is that you are disconnected from each other despite your togetherness. It is also one reason why a lot of women turn to other women for those channels of support.
>
> You are afraid to acknowledge how much you need each other in that way. As if it's some kind of failing or weakness on your part. But it's mutual, and that is what humans have forgotten. You have forgotten because you were taught wrong as women, as being insignificant. It was like two tongues: on one side is a desperation to have access to the women's capacity to draw those energies; on the other, you're deemed as not that important. In all of these confusing mixed messages you have forgotten who you are.

Beauty shows me an image of a gathering of women in a circle. I think she is suggesting ways women can begin to heal through mutual support. I am reminded that some men are doing this too: my husband is involved in men's circles that support one another's reclaiming of their authentic masculine energy.

> For human women to restore and rebalance these energies they are going to need each to remember who they are. It's not about separating from those who carry the masculine; it's about remembering, so that when women are in the presence of those who carry the masculine energies, they

will be able to make those exchanges from their deeper awareness of themselves, rather than out of weakness and fear. These exchanges are not always sexual. That is just one way that they are transmitted.

Beauty stresses this last point. Juano the stallion, she is saying, continues to provide a masculine flow of energy in the direction of the mares, for the whole herd. (This subject came up during my previous visit.)

He might look to you like he is standing in the field doing nothing, but he is working a lot, pretty much all the time. The herd could not do the healing work we are asked to do with humans without what Juano is doing for us. If you don't believe me, look at a herd that doesn't have a stallion. They won't be able to do this kind of healing work. Because part of what the stallions do is to energetically support the geldings and the mares.

Beauty's focus shifts to the herd.

The reason the herd gets tired is not because you work us hard, but because we provide energy to the people who come here and ride us. It's hard because the horse will send the energy and it goes right out of the person. So they send it again and the supporting, healing energy flows, but it just doesn't reach people in a way they can absorb. Eventually people open, and they begin to release their blocks and receive the flow, and it supports them for the time they are here. After they leave and are disconnected from the herd, if they want to keep feeling well they will have to come back, or else figure out how to tap into those energetic flows somewhere else. So the mares need Juano to support them in the masculine, which then comingles with their feminine, to provide full energetic support to the people with whom the horses are working.

Beauty pauses, and is very silent and standing very still. I feel something shift. I feel different; emotional in a way that I had not been feeling, with a sense of sorrow, of looming catastrophe, something very serious is coming up. I am hearing the word foolishness repeated: foolishness, foolishness. Beauty begins again:

> The way that the male and the female in human communities have considered each other unworthy, or not of value, or not needed, this rugged independence and separation, is the same thing that has happened with your divided awareness of and beliefs about the earth. You have lost sight of our mutual dependence on and need of it. It is a fragmentation, a split, a separating from your core source in Earth and each other. It will not continue this way.

I begin to cry as I feel myself shift deeper into the flow of communication with her:

> Some of you are going crazy, and this separation is why. Most humans are unaware of how much they are connected to the earth. Just look. All the symptoms of that ignorance are right in front of you. The violence is part of it. And though these new symptoms are dramatic, their roots are ancient.

"What are we to do?" asks Sally, a woman from England who has joined us from the workshop.

There is nothing you can do to change the course of events for humanity as a whole, or where this is leading. But there is a lot you can do as individuals to survive the major changes that are coming.

"What major changes?" I wonder. But I am not of a mind to ask, feeling overwhelmed by the waves of emotion.

The reason some of the horses in this herd are here is to help you. You are going to need the animals to help you remember, so that you can survive and be okay.

I am beginning to weep but am still able to translate and speak what I am hearing Beauty say:

People have to get this or it's going to be chaos.

"Is she suggesting that we have to prepare ourselves?" one of the women asks.

Another comments, "We have to heal the earth."

I reply, "The earth is fine. It's powerful and intelligent. Once we are gone, it will heal itself and be just fine."

"Why are you weeping?" Debbie asks me.

"Because Beauty says it's already started. She is telling us that Earth is alive and intelligent and that it wants all of life to thrive, but we humans are compromising that. So it's going to do what it has to in order to protect the whole of life."

Another woman asks, "You mean it will get rid of us?"

"I am not sure. Shall I can ask Beauty?" I return. This I do, and her response is,

> Earth is already in the process of doing that. The process has already started. There will be a great deal of suffering. The earth is shifting and soon will not be hospitable to humans.

"What are you being called to do, Rosa?" Debbie asks me, thinking that Beauty will know.

I had been thinking my call is to write what I learn from the horses, but I did not expect this kind of message from Beauty.

The spring after Bill and I met, we travelled together to New York City. It happened to be Easter weekend, although neither of us was there for religious purposes. (In fact, Bill and I have left formal religious observances behind, each for our own reasons. Neither of us had Easter on our minds.) We decide to visit The Cloisters, a museum run by the Metropolitan Museum of Art, which holds an extensive collection of art, architecture, and artifacts from Medieval Europe, most of which are religious icons. When we arrive we learn of an afternoon concert of sacred choral music performance by the a cappella group, Pomerium. They'd be singing in the Fuentidueña Chapel, a reconstructed 12th-century space built of more than 3000 heavy limestone blocks. We buy tickets for the concert.

The half-dome ceiling was decorated with religious imagery, and a 12th-century painted Spanish wood crucifix hung from the arch. As Bill and I sat quietly listening to the singing, I gazed up at the cross. I found no inspiration in what it represented, a punishing reminder of the life of a great spiritual master who had apparently "died for our sins." It failed to move me. The music, however, was mesmerizing, and led me into a peaceful state of mind. A while later, I looked up again at the cross, its Jesus figure hanging with outstretched arms and the exposed ribs of an emaciated man. I then heard the still small voice within me say,

> *See me for what I am. I am alive in you. The crucifixion repre-*
> *sents a mistaken belief that the I am, the most sacred part of your*
> *being, can be destroyed. Yes, the body is lost, along with the ego-self*
> *that was identified with it. But the image above you and the resur-*
> *rection celebrated today, simply mean that the I am, the eternal*
> *living Presence of God, cannot be destroyed. Let this experience*
> *be a reminder that through grace and divine love you always have*
> *the opportunity to let that Presence be resurrected and rise within*
> *you, that you may live as you are truly are meant to be.*

Now four years have passed since that Cloisters visit, and it's almost a year since my sobering encounter with the mare named Beauty. I wait and watch in anticipation of the suffering Beauty has predicted will come to humanity. Every new catastrophe gives me pause: extreme weather; failures of communication systems; random gun violence; threats of epidemics involving viruses and bacteria; proliferations of invasive plant species; droughts and insect anomalies. I wonder, is it happening already, is the earth displacing the human species? Are Earth's systems changing in ways that are disturbing to human life? Recalling that moment in the Cloisters helps me take in Beauty's devastating news. It helps me remember the crucial truth that change and death are inevitable on the material plane—but also that our true identity, the eternal Presence of that which is, is indestructible. Whatever perils we face in the coming years, I know that the Presence, the same force that life has shown me time and again, will live on forever. I also remember that Beauty conveyed that while dire, this situation is not inevitable; there is still an opportunity for us to change our consciousness as Earth changes, to live in closer alignment with the life force of Earth. We humans are "cherished" on Earth, as Beauty expressed. But our free will leaves our decision to us.

At times I feel helpless to do anything that will make a difference, other than to write what I have learned from my own journey, and from the horses who say they are here to help humanity. Can these animals help us? I think yes; they point us to the same eternal Presence I felt at the Cloisters. They and other animals can help us to remember who we truly are meant to be. But first we must be willing to shift our awareness in order to experience the Presence from within, and from that place to embrace the fullness of our interconnected being here on Earth.

I write this conclusion from a cabin in a 300-acre woodland preserve on secluded Wild Goose Pond in rural New Hampshire. On our last day there, I circumnavigated the lake alone by kayak. Moving along the forested shoreline, I notice the darkness among the hemlocks, the blueberry bushes readying next years' buds, the water hyacinth and lotus blossoms. Other than one other person on the water, busily practicing his sculling skills, my only companion on the water is a single common loon. Seeing her at a distance, I paddle the kayak quietly in her direction; the only sounds the lapping of water against the hull, and an owl's long hoots across the still water. Drawing close, I begin a prayer:

Great Mother, appearing to me in the form of this loon, I approach you with the desire to learn and to understand. Please allow me to come close enough to watch, to be near so that I may feel the life force in you.

I drift even closer, still my paddles and focus on my breath. With each exhalation I release myself further, and further letting go of all expectations. Dropping my personal, ego need for a particular experience, I let go of everything except the awareness of being in her presence. I inhale, aware that I am. And so is she. That is enough, and in that is everything.

Epilogue

I visited Costa Rica again in January 2016, six months after I'd completed this manuscript. I went into the pasture where Beauty and the rest of the herd roam freely when not on trail rides, participating in equine facilitated workshops, or being fed and groomed in the barn. I stood there quietly on a grassy knoll, in a meditative state of mind, simply being among eleven or so geldings, mares, and foals. Other horses, including Beauty, were grazing in the field below. When the horse named Conan approached me, I spoke to him with affection and gratitude for the support he has given me and other humans. After a few minutes Beauty meandered by, first seeming disinterested, then standing alone on a muddy path. I went to her; she turned to look at me. She was the first to speak.

"You've changed."

"Yes, I feel different inside," I replied. Together, and in silence, for another five minutes or so, Beauty and I stood side by side, my hand resting gently on her back.

"Finally; you are centered and whole in yourself."

I stroked her neck feeling connected to her, but without the sense of longing I'd had in previous visits with her. Indeed, I had changed. "Yes, Beauty; I am at peace," I tell her. "I can feel the love of the life force that connects you and me, and all living species of the earth. So thank you, Beauty. Now I am awake.

About the Author

ROSALYN W. BERNE, PH.D. explores the intersecting realms between emerging technologies, science, fiction, and myth, and between the human and non-human worlds. As a university professor she writes and teaches about engineering and technology in society and the ethical implications of technological development, often using science fiction material in her classes. In her personal life she continues to discover the transformational nature of human-equine relationships, and offers facilitation and translation services for enhancing communication between horses and their owners. She is author of *Nanotalk: Conversations with Scientists and Engineers About Ethics, Meaning, and Belief in the Development of Nanotechnology* (Earlbaum Press, 2005) and the novel *Waiting in the Silence* (Spore Press, 2012). The sequel to that novel, *Walking on the Sea,* is currently underway. *Creating Life from Life: Biotechnology and Science Fiction* brings the non-fictional writing of research scientists together with Berne's science fiction short stories (Pan Stanford Publishing, 2014). *Waking to Beauty* is the sequel to *When the Horses Whisper* (2013). In it Rosalyn continues her exploration of the human-animal interconnection, and delves more deeply into her psychic gifts.

Related Titles

If you enjoyed *Waking to Beauty*, you may also enjoy other Rainbow Ridge titles. Read more about them at *www.rainbowridgebooks.com*.

When the Horses Whisper: The Wisdom of Wise and Sentient Beings
by Rosalyn W. Berne

The Cosmic Internet: Explanations from the Other Side
by Frank DeMarco

Conversations with Jesus: An Intimate Journey
by Alexis Eldridge

Dialogue with the Devil: Enlightenment for the Unwilling
by Yves Patak

The Divine Mother Speaks: The Healing of the Human Heart by Rashmi
Khilnani

Difficult People: A Gateway to Enlightenment
by Lisette Larkins

When Do I See God: Finding the Path to Heaven
by Jeff Ianniello

Dance of the Electric Hummingbird
by Patricia Walker

Coming Full Circle: Ancient Teachings for a Modern World
by Lynn Andrews

Thank Your Wicked Parents
by Richard Bach

The Buddha Speaks: To the Buddha Nature Within
by Rashmi Khilnani

*Consciousness: Bridging the Gap Between Conventional Science
and the New Super Science of Quantum Mechanics*
by Eva Herr

Jesusgate: A History of Concealment Unraveled
by Ernie Bringas

Messiah's Handbook: Reminders for the Advanced Soul
by Richard Bach

Blue Sky, White Clouds
by Eliezer Sobel

Inner Vegas: Creating Miracles, Abundance, and Health
by Joseph Gallenberger, Ph.D.

*Your Soul Remembers: Accessing Your
Past Lives through Soul Writing*
by Joanne DiMaggio

Lessons in Courage: Peruvian Shamanic Wisdom for Everyday Life
by Bonnie Glass-Coffin, Ph.D.
and don Oscar Miro-Quesada

Rainbow Ridge Books publishes spiritual, metaphysical, and self-help titles, and is distributed by Square One Publishers in Garden City Park, New York.

To contact authors and editors, peruse our titles, and see submission guidelines, please visit our website at *www.rainbowridgebooks.com*.

For orders and catalogs, please call toll-free:
(877) 900-BOOK.